JOSEPH

Terry Hyman's book on the life of Joseph paints a vibrant picture of God's master plan at work in a fractured family. Even those who have spent many hours reading, meditating, and teaching from these narrative chapters in Genesis will find Pastor Hyman has an eye for helpful analysis as well as practical application. His work is insightful and thought-provoking. You will find his pastor's heart behind every astute observation and personal challenge he draws out of the text. The book functions well as a handbook for understanding the message of Genesis 37-50—both as a help for academic exegetical study and for encouraging a rich devotional time with the Lord. I often found myself pausing to consider my own character and how I was responding to the things God had brought into my life. The book is more than a commentary or character study; it is the unfolding and application of God's Word directly from the pages of Holy Scripture.

Marshall Fant IV, Senior Pastor
Harvest Baptist Church, Rock Hill, SC

We live in a day characterized by individuals, media, and masses demanding 'equity' while disregarding justice and seeking to destroy justice (Rom. 10:3). It is easy and too common in such an environment for many Christians to lose the joy, peace, and power of God by becoming frustrated and bitter. Brother Hyman has soundly and clearly expounded in this book the testimony given to us in God's Word of the life of Joseph with the biblical principles for every believer to be able to grow and serve, regardless of the social and political setting.

Lonny Schmid
Retired missionary

I have had the honor of previewing the manuscript of Terry Hyman's recent book, *Joseph: The Godly Perspective of a Mistreated Man*. The work is not intended to be a detailed commentary; but rather, it is a warm, devotional, careful look at the biblical account of the life of the patriarch Joseph. My heart was warmed and, at times, convicted by the simple review of the life of Joseph. I appreciated that the author did not hide the human flaws that, on occasion, surface in Joseph's life. While it is clear that Joseph is overwhelmingly a model of godliness, Terry Hyman does not paint Joseph as the "perfect man" with no recorded failures. Even though this work is a rather brief overview, I was struck by the notice given to some often-overlooked details in the biblical story of Joseph. Some of these 'little things' are shown to have importance in understanding the motives and later decisions Joseph or his family members made. I can wholeheartedly recommend this book both for those who know very little about the biblical account of Joseph and those who have known and studied the story many times. There is abundant application to struggles with bitterness and resentment that Joseph helps us understand. Joseph is a striking proof that God enables His children to overcome the vortex of defeat and negativity produced by a self-focused, unforgiving spirit.

Clint Jeffcott
Retired pastor

Joseph: The Godly Perspective of a Mistreated Man is a classic book that gives a 'play-by-play' account of what happened to a man who was misused, misunderstood, and maliciously accused. Terry Hyman does an incredible job explaining and applying the biblical principles that were evident in Joseph's journey as he navigated some of the toughest circumstances life could offer. This book is a must-read for those who enjoy practical truths that apply to everyday living.

Rusty Smith, Senior Pastor
Mikado Baptist Church, Macon, GA

intended to be a detailed commentary; but rather, it is a warm, devotional, careful look at the biblical account of the life of the patriarch Joseph. My heart was warmed and, at times, convicted by the simple review of the life of Joseph. I appreciated that the author did not hide the human flaws that, on occasion, surface in Joseph's life. While it is clear that Joseph is overwhelmingly a model of godliness, Terry Hyman does not paint Joseph as the "perfect man" with no recorded failures. Even though this work is a rather brief overview, I was struck by the notice given to some often-overlooked details in the biblical story of Joseph. Some of these 'little things' are shown to have importance in understanding the motives and later decisions Joseph or his family members made. I can wholeheartedly recommend this book both for those who know very little about the biblical account of Joseph and those who have known and studied the story many times. There is abundant application to struggles with bitterness and resentment that Joseph helps us understand. Joseph is a striking proof that God enables His children to overcome the vortex of defeat and negativity produced by a self-focused, unforgiving spirit.

Clint Jeffcott
Retired pastor

Joseph: The Godly Perspective of a Mistreated Man is a classic book that gives a 'play-by-play' account of what happened to a man who was misused, misunderstood, and maliciously accused. Terry Hyman does an incredible job explaining and applying the biblical principles that were evident in Joseph's journey as he navigated some of the toughest circumstances life could offer. This book is a must-read for those who enjoy practical truths that apply to everyday living.

Rusty Smith, Senior Pastor
Mikado Baptist Church, Macon, GA

T E R R Y   W .   H Y M A N

JOSEPH

The Godly Perspective of a Mistreated man

AMBASSADOR INTERNATIONAL
GREENVILLE, SOUTH CAROLINA & BELFAST, NORTHERN IRELAND

www.ambassador-international.com

Joseph

The Godly Perspective of a Mistreated Man

ISBN: 978-1-64960-890-1, hardcover
ISBN: 978-1-64960-609-9, paperback
eISBN: 978-1-64960-660-0

Edited by Emily Caseres
Cover Design by Hannah Linder Designs
Interior Typesetting by Dentelle Design

All Scripture quotations are taken from the King James Version of the Bible. Public Domain.

AMBASSADOR INTERNATIONAL
Emerald House
411 University Ridge, Suite B14
Greenville, SC 29601
United States
www.ambassador-international.com

AMBASSADOR BOOKS
The Mount
2 Woodstock Link
Belfast, BT6 8DD
Northern Ireland, United Kingdom
www.ambassadormedia.co.uk

The colophon is a trademark of Ambassador, a Christian publishing company.

God orchestrates worldly events according to His divine wisdom
and directs the movements of men to accomplish His purpose and plan.

CONTENTS

FOREWORD

IN THIS BOOK, THE AUTHOR has captured the life of Joseph for us in the most exceptional and practical way. He has systematically laid out the proofs of his proposition that Joseph was a godly man who was maliciously mistreated in the cruelest ways imaginable. As he draws these out of the book of Genesis, Brother Hyman points out several benchmarks that reveal how Joseph remained faithful to the Word of God and retained his integrity under the most arduous circumstances any human being can be put through.

Any serious readers who want biblical answers on how to respond to the mistreatment and manipulation of others (even family members) will find a wellspring of applications from the life of Joseph that will help them respond correctly to rejection, slander, and false accusations.

I found this book rich with practical truths from one of the most abused men in the Bible. In the culture in which we live today that constantly cries out for equality, impartiality, and fairness, Brother Hyman points to the inner (spiritual) characteristics of Joseph that were put in his heart by his God, who brought him through his rejection and loneliness.

I found this book refreshing and rich with practical applications that help the reader develop an acceptance of the sovereignty of God, Who is able to use the tragedies in our lives for His good and glory.

Dr. Rick Arrowood
Executive Director, Slavic Baptist Mission

INTRODUCTION

LIFE IS TOUGH! AROUND EVERY corner, behind every bush, and just over every hill, there seems to await some new challenge to our belief that life rewards those who do the right things. As children, we were taught that integrity was indispensable, that character demanded kindness and generosity, and that doing right would be rewarded; but it often seems that life teaches exactly the opposite. Repeatedly, those who are guilty seem to benefit from their wrongs. They not only go free but are also compensated with unthinkable popularity and prosperity. Meanwhile, those who live honorably seem to struggle. We have come to the distasteful, though accurate, conclusion that life is not fair.

Is it possible that fairness is overrated? Could it be that we have established an impossible goal for society, wrongly equating the concept of "fairness" with "justice?" Joseph must have thought so. He never seemed to flinch at the unfair challenges that characterized his life—and there were many. Repeatedly, he responded to those challenges with patience and faith, demonstrating an extraordinary sense of confidence that things were going to turn out right in the end. It was almost like he anticipated their arrival, embracing them as mere inconvenient steps in the process of achieving God's will for his life.

Although justice and fairness are usually treated as synonyms, they have very different values. Justice can only be achieved by means of righteous judgment. Fairness has no such limitation. As long as every individual is treated equally, fairness can be achieved without regard for moral integrity.

For example, thieves often require complete trust and absolute fairness within their ranks, yet their pursuits are characterized by injustice. People often demand fairness without concern for justice. Indeed, justice actually impedes their pursuit of fairness. They are driven by a desire to profit from the perceived benefits of "fairness" and will never agree to operate within the boundaries of "justice." Their moral code will not permit it.

Yet Joseph was a man driven by a non-negotiable commitment to righteousness; and he never stopped to consider the cost, which was often devastating. He embraced a clear biblical principle that gave him the supernatural endurance necessary to persevere in the face of adversity, along with the certainty that justice would prevail. Abraham, while interceding for the people of Sodom, asked the question, "Shall not the Judge of all the earth do right?" (Gen. 18:25). Moses answered the question in Deuteronomy 32:4 when he said, "He is the Rock, his work is perfect: for all his ways are judgment: a God of truth and without iniquity, just and right is he." Joseph knew Abraham's God; he valued justice above fairness; and he was convinced that "the Judge of all the earth" would "do right." That assurance allowed Joseph to see his life from a heavenly angle. He knew that his God was in control. Though mistreated, he persevered—because he viewed life from a godly perspective.

CHAPTER 1

THE BEGINNING

GENESIS 30-35

NO ACCOUNT OF JOSEPH'S LIFE can be considered complete without a thorough examination of his family. It was the unusual circumstances surrounding Joseph's birth that provided the foundation for all that happened to him. The story begins in Genesis 30:22-24: "And God remembered Rachel, and God hearkened to her and opened her womb. And she conceived, and bare a son; and said, God hath taken away my reproach: and she called his name Joseph; and said, The LORD SHALL ADD TO ME ANOTHER SON."

Joseph was the eleventh of twelve sons of Jacob. His mother was Rachel, the second wife of his father. His older brothers were half-brothers. Reuben, Simeon, Levi, and Judah were all born to Jacob's first wife, Leah. God had chosen to favor her since Jacob didn't (Gen. 29:31). God had also allowed Rachel to remain barren. Dan and Naphtali were born to Rachel's handmaid Bilhah, the result of Rachel's envy and manipulation (Gen. 30:1-8). The next two sons, Gad and Asher, were birthed by Zilpah, Leah's handmaid. Two other sons were born before Joseph, Issachar and Zebulon, both to Leah. Finally, Joseph also had a younger, full-blooded brother, Benjamin (Gen. 35:16-20).

Joseph's birth brought great joy. He was the first child born to Rachel. Though she was Jacob's second wife, she was his first love. Jacob had been the unknowing victim of an insidious scheme concocted and executed by his uncle Laban (Gen. 29:1-30). The original agreement was that Jacob would serve Laban for seven years in exchange for his younger daughter Rachel. Instead, Jacob spent more than twenty years with Laban; and when his service was complete, he had two wives, one of his choosing and one that he gained as a consequence of Laban's deception. The result was a family in turmoil, filled with anger, bitterness, envy, and distrust. The conflicts were fostered by two wives, four mothers, and twelve sons, all competing for the attention and favor of one man, who was likewise the product of an equally dysfunctional family.

The situation was made even more stressful because of Jacob's attitude toward his eleventh son. Joseph held favored status with his father. This unfairness in the family caused strong resentment among the older brothers, essentially destroying any hope for building meaningful, productive relationships among the siblings.

JOSEPH'S CHARACTER

Can you imagine for a second what life must have been like for Joseph as a boy? He was living in a household with eleven other young men, a third of whom were born to women who were described as "handmaids." Handmaids were female servants. As handmaids, Bilhah and Zilpah were charged with the responsibility of attending to the personal needs of Rachel and Leah respectively. While their legal standing changed when they became "wives" of Jacob, they retained a somewhat inferior status in the family. They were still Rachel and Leah's handmaids. When the report was given of Jacob's sons in Genesis 35:23-26, the mothers of Dan, Naphtali, Gad, and Asher were identified as handmaids of Rachel and Leah rather than wives of Jacob. It is certain that their sons noticed the discrepancy.

Children observe and remember far more than we anticipate, and those observations have an influence. What they see in the lives of their parents has far more impact than what they hear from them. Joseph was perhaps five or six years old when Jacob finally left Haran to begin his journey back to Bethel. What Joseph observed over the next eleven years helped to shape his character and prepare him for the challenges he was destined to face.

THE IMPORTANCE OF FORGIVENESS

Joseph's first lesson dealt with the importance of forgiveness, and the lesson came from an unexpected source. For years, Jacob had been living with a heavy burden of guilt, a consequence of his deceptive practices toward his brother, Esau. He had been able to disregard it because he was living and working in a distant land. Now he was returning home, and it became obvious that soon he would have to face his brother. Fear began to swell in the heart of Jacob as he contemplated such a meeting. How could he ever forget the words of warning he received from his mother as she encouraged him to flee?

> Behold, thy brother Esau, as touching thee, doth comfort himself, purposing to kill thee. Now therefore, my son, obey my voice; and arise, flee thou to Laban my brother to Haran; And tarry with him a few days, until thy brother's fury turn away; Until thy brother's anger turn away from thee, and he forget that which thou hast done to him: then I will send, and fetch thee from thence: why should I be deprived also of you both in one day? (Gen. 27:42-45)

Now Jacob had to face his brother. So in keeping with his nature, he tried every scheme he could think of to soften Esau's heart and demonstrate his penitence. He sent messengers ahead bearing gifts and pleading for grace. He spent the evening before the meeting wrestling with God. Then, as Jacob approached his brother, he called him "lord" and bowed repeatedly before him. The encounter, however, went much better than Jacob anticipated. The bitterness and hatred he expected wasn't there. Instead, Esau seemed genuinely glad to see him. Genesis 33:4 says that "Esau ran to meet him, and embraced him, and fell on his neck, and kissed him: and they wept."

Somehow, Esau's attitude had changed. It was most evident when Jacob explained that the gifts he had sent were meant to provide restitution for his past offenses. Esau refused Jacob's offering, stating emphatically, "I have enough, my brother; keep that thou hast unto thyself" (Gen. 33:9). Jacob's debt was forgiven; his trespass was forgotten; and his relationship with Esau was restored. Forgiveness has been described as "removing your hands from the neck of your enemy." In Matthew 5:43-44, Jesus taught his disciples about forgiveness: "Ye have heard that it hath been said, Thou shalt love thy neighbour, and hate thine enemy. But I say unto you, Love your enemies, bless them that curse you, do good to them that hate you, and pray for them which despitefully use you, and persecute you." That's exactly what Esau did. He made a conscious choice to forgive his brother.

Strangely enough, Jacob was not the only one who was aided by Esau's change of heart. Joseph saw in Esau's attitude an important scriptural principle that later in life would become a central element of his character. He learned the importance of forgiveness.

THE EMPTY SATISFACTION OF UNRESTRAINED VENGEANCE

Joseph's second lesson came as a result of his father's carelessness. Jacob got sidetracked. Instead of continuing his journey back to the "land of his fathers" in obedience to God's clear command (Gen. 31:3), he stopped to settle down in Succoth (Gen. 33:17-20). He established a residence there, building a house for his family and barns for his cattle. He then moved on to Shalem, a city in Shechem, where he bought a piece of land and again settled down. It's never a wise choice when a believer decides to take a detour from the will of God. Jacob's pause, however, was particularly costly, and Joseph learned an important lesson about the empty satisfaction of unrestrained vengeance.

It's hard to understand what must have been going through Jacob's mind. Not only did he put his family in danger by settling down near Shalem, but he also allowed his daughter, Dinah, to explore the city alone (Gen. 34:1). She wasn't there long when she caught the eye of a handsome, young prince. Shechem, the son of Hamor the Hivite, noticed her, charmed her, and defiled her (Gen. 34:2). Perhaps Shechem deserves some benefit of the doubt in this situation. He was in his own country, operating according to the accepted customs and morality of his society. While Shechem's actions were under no circumstances defensible, Dinah and her father, Jacob, had to bear some responsibility for her vulnerability. Neither was Shechem's intent wholly without honor. Genesis 34:3-4 reveals his love for Dinah, along with a sincere desire to marry her.

Dinah's brothers, however, were not so honorable. When Hamor introduced what was, in his mind, a very generous offer to blend their cultures, Simeon and Levi responded deceitfully (Gen. 34:13). Instead of rejecting his offer outright, they chose to pretend that there was a specific tenet of their faith that had to be fulfilled before they would agree. They earnestly (and dishonestly) insisted that the removal of that obstacle would satisfy their complaint. If Hamor would agree for all of the men in Shechem to meet the Jewish requirement of circumcision, then all would be well. Shechem could marry Dinah, and they would be willing to "dwell with them" and "become one people" (Gen. 34:14-16).

While Hamor, and his son Shechem, were obviously powerful leaders and shrewd negotiators, they were overmatched in this mediation. Blinded by their greed and passion, they eagerly accepted the terms and hurried back to the city to enlist the cooperation of all the men. They were anticipating much more than wives for their sons—there was a substantial amount of wealth to be gained as well (Gen. 34:20-24). They completely overlooked the customary pain and temporary incapacitation associated with the procedure, a circumstance for which Simeon and Levi were hoping.

What happened next was a far greater offense than Shechem defiling Dinah. Simeon and Levi had set their trap; now they were ready to capture their prey.

> And it came to pass on the third day, when they were sore, that
> two of the sons of Jacob, Simeon and Levi, Dinah's brethren, took
> each man his sword, and came upon the city boldly, and slew all
> the males. And they slew Hamor and Shechem his son with the
> edge of the sword, and took Dinah out of Shechem's house, and
> went out. The sons of Jacob came upon the slain, and spoiled the
> city, because they had defiled their sister. They took their sheep,
> and their oxen, and their asses, and that which was in the city,
> and that which was in the field, And all their wealth, and all their
> little ones, and their wives took they captive, and spoiled even all
> that was in the house (Gen. 34:25-29).

Shechem's sin was despicable. He used his charm and influence to defile
a young lady who was too young and inexperienced to know what was
going on. Simeon and Levi's sin was vicious and utterly without compassion.
Shechem was driven by passionate love for Dinah. Simeon and Levi were
driven by passionate hatred for Shechem. Shechem was willing to pay any
price necessary to compensate for his sin. Simeon and Levi could not inflict
sufficient pain and suffering to satisfy their demand for vengeance. Shechem
was a Canaanite, a pagan, who knew not God. Simeon and Levi were the sons
of Jacob, a patriarch of the faith. There was no excuse for their actions.

When Simeon and Levi returned home and Jacob realized what they had
done, he was enraged. They had destroyed Jacob's testimony and placed his
family in grave danger, all because they were determined to exact revenge.
Jacob never forgot what they did. In Genesis 49:5-7, as he was addressing his
sons before he died, Jacob reminded Simeon and Levi of the severity of their
transgression—"Simeon and Levi are brethren; instruments of cruelty are in
their habitations" (v. 5)—and condemned them for their merciless slaughter
of innocent victims—"Cursed be their anger, for it was fierce; and their wrath,
for it was cruel: I will divide them in Jacob, and scatter them in Israel" (v.7).

It is important to remember that this is a study of the life of Joseph. He
watched these events unfold. There can be no doubt that what he saw helped

him to learn that unrestrained vengeance quenches no thirst and removes no hatred. It only serves to intensify the bitterness. Joseph spent most of his life as a victim of unfair treatment. Yet he never responded with seething hatred as did Simeon and Levi. I'd say he learned this lesson well.

THE UNPLEASANT REALITY OF DEATH

Life produces many heartaches—some the natural result of ignoring God's principle of sowing and reaping, others a simple consequence of life in the flesh. Sometimes, life is just unfair! Other times, it's just life. Solomon said in Ecclesiastes 3:1-2, "To every thing there is a season, and a time to every purpose under the heaven: A time to be born, and a time to die." Joseph's next lesson would come from observing the unpleasant reality of death.

After the disgusting display at Shechem, Jacob received another message from the Lord: "And God said unto Jacob, Arise, go up to Bethel, and dwell there: and make there an altar unto God, that appeared unto thee when thou fleddest from the face of Esau thy brother" (Gen. 35:1). Instead of confronting Jacob for his disobedience, God, in His mercy, reordered Jacob's steps, getting him back on track. Jacob's first stop was at Bethel to erect an altar. It was there, more than fifteen years earlier, that Jacob had dreamed of a ladder reaching to Heaven. In that dream God confirmed the promise made to his grandfather Abraham concerning the yet future nation of Israel (Gen. 28:10-19). Now Jacob built another altar at Bethel to commemorate his first encounter with God.

While there, Deborah, the nurse who cared for Rebekah, Jacob's mother, died. This is perhaps the first time Joseph actually felt the sting of death. At this point, he would have been old enough to understand the anguish of losing someone very close to the family. Although Scripture does not record the time or place of Rebekah's death, it seems likely that it occurred while Joseph was very young. Deborah would have provided a significant link to Joseph's grandmother.

On the next segment of their journey, they came to Ephrath, which was the original name of the city we now know as Bethlehem. Joseph's lesson in grief reached a new level when his mother went into labor. Childbirth in those days was especially hard. There were no hospitals with pristine birthing rooms filled with the latest lifesaving equipment. There were no incubators for babies that were born prematurely. There were no highly trained medical personnel who were aware of the most recently discovered treatments for unexpected complications. In this case, the birthing room was perhaps a cave or a tent erected hastily along the trail.

Verse sixteen says that Rachel "travailed" and had "hard labor." The fact that the midwife felt it necessary to reassure Rachel with a promise that the child would survive implied that the situation was, indeed, severe. Though the child survived, Rachel died. Joseph gained a brother and lost his mother at the same time. Somehow, I doubt that the arrival of Benjamin made up for the loss of his mother.

There was yet a third death waiting for Joseph. After dealing with another shameful deed executed by his oldest son, Reuben (Gen. 35:21-22), Jacob (now called Israel) journeyed to Mamre, to pay one final visit to his blind, sickly father. Isaac was now 180 years old. Once again, Joseph felt the bitter sting of death as his grandfather "gave up the ghost" (Gen. 35:29). In a very short period of time, Joseph lost Deborah, the closest link he had to his grandmother Rebekah, as well as his mother and his grandfather.

DISCUSSION QUESTIONS

1. Joseph was born into a family that was plagued by conflict. Envy, bitterness, strife, and anger ruled the hearts of all the sons, except Joseph. What fueled the conflict, and how did Jacob contribute to the problem? How do you think Jacob could have avoided intensifying the issue or helped to defuse it?

2. While still a child, Joseph observed three unusual situations that influenced his character in a positive way. The first had to do with forgiveness. What was the issue that created the confrontation, and how was it resolved? What principles should believers employ to resolve their differences?

3. The second situation that Joseph observed was the polar opposite of the first, dealing with vengeance instead of forgiveness. How was the consequence of the second situation different from the first? Did Simeon and Levi misinterpret the circumstances? If so, how? Did their actions result in a satisfying resolution to the conflict? If not, what could they have done to arrive at a resolution?

4. Life is not always pleasant, and Joseph faced in a very short time the deaths of three people who each held a place of great importance in his life. How did grieving their loss help prepare him for what was ahead?

CHAPTER 2
THE DECEPTION

GENESIS 37

THE NARRATIVE OF JOSEPH'S LIFE officially begins in Genesis 37. Verse two reveals that Joseph was, at age seventeen, given the responsibility of "feeding the flock with his brethren." There is nothing significant about that revelation. It was not unusual for the youngest son in a family to assume the burden of caring for the sheep. It was the most tedious, lonely, and undesirable of all chores. In this case, however, Joseph wasn't lonely. He was working with Dan, Naphtali, Gad, and Asher, the four sons of Bilhah and Zilpah, respectively. Since he was the youngest of the lot, it seems likely that he had little authority; and since he was hated by his brethren (v. 4), it is certain he was assigned the most menial tasks associated with an already distasteful job.

Whether Joseph's choice to bring an "evil report" to his father regarding his coworkers was wise is open for debate. It certainly did nothing to improve his standing with them. Nor can we be certain that the report was entirely free of ill will on Joseph's part. Many assume that Joseph had no battle with fleshly attitudes such as anger, envy, bitterness, and resentment. Yet Joseph was human. He had a sinful nature; and while he was usually able to corral those fleshly attitudes, it is irrational to assume that he never succumbed. There is a reason verse four states that his brothers "hated him, and could not speak peaceably unto him," and there was probably more to it than Jacob's "favorite son" status.

Much consideration has been given to the design, appearance, and significance of Joseph's "coat of many colors." The only thing we know for certain is that Jacob gave it to him to communicate two things: his love for Joseph and that Joseph was "the son of his old age" (v. 3). Furthermore, it was a major cause for the hatred of his brothers.

THE CAUSTIC POWER OF DREAMS

It is interesting how often dreams are mentioned in the account of Joseph's life. At seventeen, there were the dreams portraying Joseph's power and prestige. Later, when Joseph was in prison, he was challenged with interpreting the dreams of the butler and the baker; and Joseph's deliverance from prison was accomplished as a result of Pharaoh's dream. They were all of divine origin and had prophetic significance. They were a necessary part of God's plan for the nation of Israel.

Soon after this event, Scripture tells us, "And Joseph dreamed a dream" (v. 5). In fact, there were two dreams. The first portrayed Joseph as a sheaf in the field with other sheaves, symbolizing his brothers (v. 5-8). While they all stood upright, they did not all stand together. Joseph's sheaf took center stage, and his brother's sheaves "made obeisance" to his sheaf. When he chose to share that bit of information with his brothers, they responded as we would have expected them to. They were surprised and offended, and they rebuked him for his arrogance.

The second dream was very similar to the first, except that his brethren and parents were depicted by the sun, moon, and eleven stars. Again, Joseph held the place of prominence, and the others "made obeisance" to him (v. 8-11). This time, he shared his dream with his father as well as his brethren; and since Joseph did not identify the characters, there was no obvious interpretation. Only his father understood, and again, Joseph was rebuked for his egotism.

Was Joseph guilty as charged? What was Joseph thinking as he repeated the content of those dreams? Did pride corrupt his motive? Could he have taken just a bit of pleasure in revealing that he would not always be under the thumb or subject to the abuse of his brethren? Remember, Joseph is seventeen years old; and though his heart is tender toward God, it is still "deceitful above all things and desperately wicked" (Jer. 17:9). That does not prove his guilt, but it does remind us of his humanity.

Verse eleven states that "his brethren envied him." Joseph had everything they wanted and, perhaps, felt they deserved. Joseph was his father's favorite, the recipient of a special robe. As such, he was destined to receive the inheritance of the firstborn. Now he seemed to have special favor with God as well. It was too much for them to accept, and their hatred grew.

HATRED, DECEIT, AND CRUELTY

Unrestrained hatred feeds on itself, and Joseph's brothers had a hearty appetite. Everything Joseph did provided additional fuel for their bitterness. When Jacob sent Joseph to find his brothers and return with a report concerning their well-being, they were more than ready to exact their revenge.

Joseph found them in Dothan. But their focus wasn't on the sheep they were tending. They were preoccupied with their bitterness toward Joseph; and when they saw him coming in the distance, they quickly finalized their plan. Verses eighteen through twenty provide the details.

First, their plan was *premeditated*, the result of seething animosity that had been growing for years. This was no impulsive decision. They had, for some time, been seeking an opportunity to release their pent-up wrath on Joseph. His visit in this remote location provided the perfect opportunity.

Next, their plan was *precautionary,* a consequence of their uncertainty about the prophetic nature of his dreams. Joseph's brothers hated him because of his dreams, but there was a subtle sense of fear associated with their actions. Verse twenty provides a glimpse of their anxiety. There was at least a slight possibility that his dreams could come true. If that happened, they would find themselves in an unacceptable position of servitude to their younger brother. The only way to eliminate the threat was to eliminate the "dreamer."

Finally, their plan was *pitiless,* evidence of a lack of concern for their father, Jacob, as well as their hated younger brother. Only Reuben understood the gravity of what they were about to do, and his influence was limited by his unstable character (Gen. 49:3-4). Rather than insisting that Joseph be allowed to go free, he sought to appease his brothers by offering an alternative that would buy him some time, permitting him to rescue Joseph later. His compromise spared Joseph's life, but it did nothing to lessen his father's grief.

Jacob loved Joseph because he was "the son of his old age" (Gen. 37:3). He had labored fourteen years for Rachel's hand in marriage and waited another twenty-seven years for the Lord to open Rachel's womb. Joseph was, indeed, a special blessing to Jacob. Losing him was almost unbearable.

Having convinced his brothers to cast Joseph into a dried-up well, Reuben went about his business, only to return to the pit and find Joseph gone. Scripture doesn't tell us where Reuben went or what he was doing. We only know that in his absence, Joseph's fate was decided.

Judah was now the spokesman. His plan would rid them of Joseph's annoying presence while preserving his life. The Midianite merchantmen that were passing by would do nicely. They would sell their brother to the Ishmaelites and let them determine Joseph's ultimate fate. Doing so would allow them to deny responsibility for any physical harm that came to their younger brother. They were certain that Joseph would end up in servitude; and since he was going to Egypt, the chance of anyone knowing what they did was negligible. Thus, their evil dealings with their brother would never be discovered.

When Reuben learned what his brothers had done, he was rattled. The Bible tells us that he "rent his clothes" (Gen. 37:29), displaying his grief and despair. Upon catching up with the perpetrators, he cried in anguish, "The child is not; and I, whither shall I go" (v. 30). At this point, he did not know whether Joseph was alive or dead. He only knew that Joseph was not where he left him and that his brothers were somehow responsible.

Now, they had to come up with an explanation for Joseph's disappearance. It would not do to pretend that Joseph had forsaken his duties and simply wandered away to seek his fortune elsewhere; he was too loyal to his father for that to be credible. Nor could they tell the truth. So they did some dreaming of their own, coming up with a story that explained Joseph's absence while implying that they were not involved: "And they took Joseph's coat, and killed a kid of the goats, and dipped the coat in the blood, And they sent the coat of many colours, and they brought it to their father; and said, This have we found: know now whether it be thy son's coat or no" (Gen. 37:31-32).

Their father was devastated! There was no question concerning the authenticity of the coat. It was unique, made especially for Joseph; and Jacob quickly came to the conclusion his sons were seeking: "It is my son's coat; an evil beast hath devoured him; Joseph is without doubt rent in pieces" (Gen. 37:33). He never stopped to consider Joseph's dreams. He never asked his sons where they found the coat. He didn't even inquire as to why the coat was not torn. If a wild beast had devoured him, surely the coat would have been shredded as well as blood-stained. And what about his body or bones? How could he be sure that Joseph was dead? Instead, he began a personal funeral dirge that lasted for more than twenty-three years.

Meanwhile, the Midianites transported Joseph to Egypt and sold him to a man named Potiphar, who was an officer of Pharaoh and captain of the guard.

DISCUSSION QUESTIONS

1. Joseph spent his early years in the fields caring for sheep with several of his brothers. How would you describe the relationship that Joseph had with his brothers?

2. Joseph's dreams played an important part in God's plan for his life. Those same dreams, however, caused a great deal of anguish within his family—first with his brothers and then with his father. How did Joseph's brothers interpret the dreams? What was Jacob's reaction to Joseph's second dream? Did Joseph bear any responsibility for their conclusions? Verse eleven says that Joseph's brethren "envied" him. In what way did that emotion affect their treatment of their brother?

3. When Jacob sent Joseph to check on his brothers (he finally caught up with them in Dothan), he received a hostile welcome. His brothers had already seen him coming and devised a plan to deal with him. What part did their hatred play in their decision? How did fear influence them?

4. The initial decision the brothers made was to "slay" Joseph (v. 18). What happened and who intervened to keep them from carrying out that sentence?

5. What did their ultimate decision reveal about their attitude toward their father? How did their father respond when he saw Joseph's coat?

CHAPTER 3

THE HYPOCRISY

GENESIS 38

IT MAY APPEAR AT FIRST reading that the events recorded in Genesis 38 have no relevance to the life of Joseph. Chapter thirty-seven ends with Joseph being sold to Potiphar, and chapter thirty-nine begins with Potiphar taking Joseph home. Why has the story of Joseph been interrupted so abruptly?

While this book is focused on the life of Joseph, we must remember that the Scriptures we are examining are actually a history of the life of Jacob, Joseph's father. Genesis 37:2 begins with the statement, "These are the generations of Jacob." As we continue our study, we will become well acquainted with Joseph's circumstances, challenges, and reactions; but we must not lose sight of the underlying truth that Joseph is simply the instrument God is using to help establish a nation that will begin with Jacob and become the primary focus of God's attention. It is this nation that the Lord will use to fulfill his promise to send the Messiah. Later in Scripture, the Messiah will be referred to as "the Lion of the tribe of Judah" (Rev. 5:5). Judah is the central character of the story found in Genesis 38. That understanding makes Genesis 38 relevant to the life of Joseph.

We are not told how much time had passed since Joseph was sold into slavery; but at some point, Judah left his brothers and became friends with a man named Hirah, a resident of Canaan. At this time, Canaan was considered a pagan land to Jacob and his family. Genesis 37:1 tells us Isaac, Jacob's father, though living in the land of Canaan, was a stranger there. Esau, Jacob's brother, had taken two wives of the Canaanite people, who were "a grief of mind" to his parents (Gen. 26:34-35). Now Judah, Joseph's brother, had also taken a Canaanite wife who bore him three sons: Er, Onan, and Shelah (Gen. 38:1-5).

Judah, following the custom of his people, arranged for his oldest son, Er, to marry a woman named Tamar. Er's legacy in Scripture is brief and ugly. Scripture does not reveal the sin of which Er was guilty, other than to say he "was wicked in the sight of the Lord" (v. 7). The offense must have been severe because the Lord took his life.

Once again, Judah followed the custom of his people and gave Tamar to his second son, Onan, to become his wife and raise children with him. Onan refused and committed an equally offensive sin, and the Lord took his life (v. 8-10). So far, Judah had given Tamar to two of his sons, and the Lord had taken them both. His remaining son, Shelah, was still rather young; and Judah was understandably hesitant about giving Tamar to him, fearing that the Lord may take him as well.

Meanwhile, Tamar was still without children, and the custom had not changed. She was expecting Judah to give her to Shelah so that he could provide her with children. Judah bought some time by promising Tamar that she would be given to Shelah as soon as he reached the appropriate age. Until that time arrived, she was to return to her father's house and wait, maintaining her status as a widow. While waiting, Judah's wife died; and he reunited with his Canaanite friend Hirah. They took a journey to Timnath to shear his sheep (v. 12).

When Tamar learned what her father-in-law was doing, she determined to set an insidious trap for him. Why would she do such a thing? She had a motive; and in her mind, what she was about to do was justified. For a woman to be childless in those days was a reproach, and Tamar believed that Judah was to blame. Neither of his sons had fulfilled their obligation; and Judah had refused to give her to his third son, even though he had reached an acceptable age. While Judah was blaming Tamar for the deaths of his sons, Tamar blamed Judah for her childless state.

Judah, in each choice he made regarding this unpleasant incident, had violated several spiritual and ethical tenets of his faith. He first married a Canaanite woman, then took a Canaanite wife for his sons. When his first two sons died because they refused to go in unto Tamar, Judah determined not to put his third son at risk. If that was not sufficient, he neglected his responsibility to care for Tamar by sending her back to dwell with her father. Each of those things was cause for public scorn in Jewish culture, and it is certain that Tamar felt the effects of that scorn.

TAMAR'S DECEPTION

In Genesis 27, we find Jacob, Judah's father, disguising himself to deceive his father, Isaac, while stealing his brother Esau's blessing. Tamar's trap for Judah was baited in the same fashion but had a very different goal. If things went according to her plan, she would accomplish several objectives. She would humiliate and punish her father-in-law publicly for his dishonesty and the casual dismissal of an unwanted burden for which he was responsible. She would remove the reproach of being childless. And she would produce at least one child (son) who would give her some security in old age.

Tamar had been living with her father for a significant amount of time and was still wearing the garments of her bereavement. She removed her mourning garments, put on a veil, and dressed in such a way that she would be mistaken for a harlot. Then she found a place beside the road to Timnath and waited.

Tamar's disguise was every bit as effective as Jacob's. As Judah passed by, he saw her, desired her, and made an offer to procure her services. Like his father and many of his brothers, he had little respect for the standards of honesty or morality. He was driven by a desire to please his flesh and had no interest in God's purpose or plan. In his mind, this would be a fleeting indulgence that would fade quickly into the realm of forgotten history. The scene is described in this way:

> When Judah saw her, he thought her to be an harlot; because she had covered her face. And he turned unto her by the way, and said, Go to, I pray thee, let me come in unto thee; (for he knew not that she was his daughter in law.) And she said, What wilt thou give me, that thou mayest come in unto me? And he said, I will send thee a kid from the flock. And she said, Wilt thou give me a pledge, till thou send it? And he said, What pledge shall I give thee? And she said, Thy signet, and thy bracelets, and thy staff that is in thine hand. And he gave it her, and came in unto her, and she conceived by him (Gen. 38:16-18).

Tamar's plan was working perfectly. The accepted price for her services was a "kid from the flock." Since Judah had no animals with him at the time, Tamar asked for a pledge from him to guarantee his payment at a later date. He readily agreed to leave with her whatever she desired, with the understanding that those items would be returned when the goat was delivered. The items she requested were very personal in nature. While the items themselves would have been quite common among prosperous men of the time, they were all very different, distinguishing certain identifying characteristics of the owner.

The first item was his signet, the ring he wore on his finger. It was the same kind of ring Pharaoh later gave to Joseph to identify him as the governor of Egypt. It demonstrated Judah's authority as head of the family. The second item was the collection of bracelets that he was wearing on his arm. They were most likely made of gold, representing his wealth. The final item was his staff, similar to a cane, with a carving at the top that was distinctly unique so that it could quickly be identified as belonging to him. Having given her the pledge, Judah conducted his "business" and went on his way, leaving the ring, bracelets, and staff with her. What he did not know was that those items would later be used to incriminate him. Tamar had convinced him that she was simply securing her payment; but in reality, she was collecting evidence to exact her revenge.

Leaving the items was not difficult for Judah. He expected them to be returned upon delivery of the goat, but retrieving them turned out to be a problem. Once again, his Canaanite friend, Hirah, served as his accomplice. He would deliver the goat and retrieve the pledge. But when he went to deliver the goat, he was unable to locate the woman. Even the men who frequented the area could not recall a harlot being there. Judah's response seemed to be a bit casual. He told Hirah to just "forget" about it. His reasoning was that if he intensified the search for her, he would be risking personal exposure. But it was not genuine guilt that influenced his decision. He was concerned about his reputation.

JUDAH'S HYPOCRISY

How easy it is for a man to convince himself of his own righteousness. Judah's incident with Tamar was now three months past, and Judah had dismissed it as if it never happened. His friends and family would certainly be offended if anyone suggested that Judah could have been involved in such an indiscretion. Judah himself would consider such an accusation to be outrageous. So his reaction to the revelation of Tamar's sin was not unexpected. It was brief, forceful, exceedingly harsh, and filled with righteous indignation: "Bring her forth, and let her be burnt" (v. 24). In his mind, such an act was reprehensible. She had "played the harlot" and brought shame and disgrace upon his family. Her punishment could not be accomplished quickly enough. He would have insisted that it be done publicly to warn others of the consequences of such depraved conduct, making sure that those observing would have no doubt about his feelings toward her behavior.

The wood was in place. The crowd had assembled. All of Jacob's brethren were there, along with their families and servants. We can be sure that the children were not excluded from this gathering. Parents would have wanted them to observe what would happen to an individual who engaged in this kind of conduct. Judah had sent servants to bring Tamar back for her punishment. When the servants arrived and told Tamar their mission, she hesitated and asked them to take a message to Judah. They took the items she gave them and the message she sent and returned them to Judah.

As the servants approached, Judah would have noticed that Tamar was not with them. When they got closer, he would have noticed that one of them was carrying something in his hands. He could not have seen the bracelets or the ring, but one item that looked like a cane would have been obvious. He looked intently as they came nearer, and his blood must have run cold when he realized that what looked like a cane was actually a shepherd's staff and that the markings on the top of it identified the staff as belonging to him. When the servants arrived, his suspicions were confirmed. They had the ring and the bracelets as well. Then came the message, "By the man whose these are, am I with child . . . Discern, I pray thee, whose these are, the signet, the bracelets and staff" (v. 25).

Judah's self-righteousness disappeared, and it was replaced with overwhelming guilt. But it was not only the guilt for having an immoral relationship with a woman he thought to be a harlot. He knew he was wrong to withhold his son Shelah from her and then put her away by sending her to live with her father. Judah was forced to face his sin, and Tamar was set free.

GOD'S PLAN

The final four verses of chapter thirty-eight give us details of the children that were born of Judah's illicit relationship with Tamar. There were twins in her womb, and the first one to be born was not the first one to make his presence known. One of the babes put his hand out, and the midwife tied a scarlet thread around it. The firstborn child, however, had no ribbon on his hand. He was named Pharez. The other child who was born second was named Zarah. The amazing thing about this situation is that God, in His sovereignty and by his grace, chose to use this union to produce the Messiah. They are all listed in Matthew 1:3, as Matthew records the lineage of Christ. Pharaz was an ancestor of Christ.

Unlike Joseph, Judah was driven by feelings rather than faith, seeking to control circumstances by his own wisdom. But God is always faithful, asserting His will to override the futile efforts of man, accomplishing His sovereign will in the process.

DISCUSSION QUESTIONS

1. Why is the story of Tamar important?

2. Two of Judah's sons had died after marrying Tamar, and he refused to give her to his third son to protect him. Doing so was a violation of a promise he had made to Tamar. Was Tamar's response (setting a trap for Judah) justified? How had Judah's refusal to give her to Shelah impact Tamar's life?

3. Judah's experience with hidden sin is a warning to every believer. Numbers 32:23 states clearly that if you sin, you can "be sure your sin will find you out." How was Judah's hypocrisy revealed?

4. When the story ends, we learn that twins were born to Tamar and that the firstborn, Pharaz was an ancestor of the Messiah. What does this story teach us about God's grace?

CHAPTER 4

THE TEMPTATION

GENESIS 39

JOSEPH'S BRETHREN HATED HIM; AND that hatred was born of anger, envy, resentment, and vindictiveness. Their intent was to invalidate Joseph's dreams and destroy his life. Sending him to Egypt in bondage satisfied their demand for vengeance while allowing them to feel somewhat proud of their generosity. Joseph was alive, but he would pay dearly for causing them such anguish. Had they followed the merchantmen to whom they sold their brother, however, and learned what happened next, they would not have been so smug.

Joseph entered Egypt in chains, but his shackles were soon removed. The Egyptian who bought Joseph had far more discernment than Joseph's brothers. It did not take him long to observe that Joseph was "a prosperous man" (Gen. 39:2). Such an assessment was hardly believable. How could he describe a man in bondage, a common slave, as prosperous?

Obviously, it wasn't Joseph's wealth that impressed Potiphar. Nor was it the clothing he wore (the robe had been taken from him and used to deceive his father). Joseph had a peculiar spirit about him, something unique that conveyed a strong sense of conviction and faith. Though Joseph was, indeed, a slave, he didn't act, think, or respond like a slave. Instead, his character was marked by encouragement and expectation. Joseph knew the Lord was in charge, and he was not going to allow himself to be swayed by negative circumstances in his life—circumstances over which he had no control—suggesting that prosperity was not an option.

Genesis 39:3 tells us what Potiphar saw in Joseph: "And his master saw that the Lord was with him and that the Lord made all that he did to prosper in his hand." Scripture doesn't reveal how long Joseph was in Potiphar's house before he was promoted to a place of authority or how much time passed before he was relieved of that responsibility. Those issues are not important. He was a slave in a foreign country, dealing with strange people and customs. While his commitment to truth served him well as he sought to build a positive relationship with his master, it became a liability when dealing with his master's wife.

SERVING DILIGENTLY

Most men in Joseph's shoes would have spent time bemoaning their ill fate. The temptation to entertain self-pity would have been too great to resist. Joseph, however, was not one to indulge such negative thoughts. Instead, he used his energy to convince Potiphar that he viewed his employment as an opportunity rather than an affliction. He was not a victim, nor was he controlled by the pain and disappointment associated with the circumstances that led him to Potiphar's house.

Joseph's strength of character provided a solid background for his consistent, faithful service. The spiritual influence in Joseph's life was obvious as well. His devotion to his God was unfaltering. Every choice he made, every word he said, every suggestion he offered was carefully fed through the sieve of God's approval. The positive results Joseph enjoyed provided sufficient evidence of God's blessing. Potiphar was watching carefully, and what he saw convinced him of Joseph's qualifications for a position of great responsibility.

Potiphar was an Egyptian officer of Pharaoh who served as captain of the guard. It is likely that he had significant wealth and property. His diverse business dealings would have required a manager who had superior negotiating skills coupled with exceptional wisdom, a combination rarely seen in the men of Egypt. When Potiphar discovered those qualities in a cheaply purchased Hebrew slave, he was overjoyed. That he could be trusted was an unexpected bonus.

Potiphar's decision to make Joseph the "overseer over his house" (Gen. 39:4) yielded immediate results: "And it came to pass from the time that he had made him overseer in his house, and over all that he had, that the Lord blessed the Egyptian's house for Joseph's sake; and the blessing of the Lord was upon all that he had in the house, and in the field" (Gen. 39:5).

DEFENDING VIRTUE

In today's world, "virtue" should be placed on the endangered values list. Because of the enormous emphasis on individual freedom to the exclusion of personal responsibility, people have lost any sense of the importance of virtue. They consider it a non-issue. Pleasure, self-gratification, and unrestrained indulgence are the accepted norms for finding happiness. Potiphar's wife would have felt right at home in the twenty-first century. She certainly knew what she wanted and was not reluctant to boldly pursue her cravings.

Verse seven says that Potiphar's wife "cast her eyes upon Joseph," indicating more than an innocent glance. In eighteenth-century vernacular, they would say that she had "set her cap" for him, meaning that she would wear apparel that included her best hat, intending to attract a certain man's attention. Potiphar's wife obviously found Joseph attractive.

Just as Joseph enjoyed favored status with his father at home, he was "well-favoured" in Potiphar's house (Gen. 39:6). The primary reason for this favor was his obvious spiritual character, although that is not what provoked the interest of Potiphar's wife. Joseph was also described as a "goodly" person, meaning that he was handsome and attractive, much like the description given of David in I Samuel 16:12. That's what caught her attention; and she did not hesitate to, nor was she subtle about, making her intentions known. Her demand is recorded in Genesis 39:7: "And it came to pass after these things, that his master's wife cast her eyes upon Joseph; and she said, Lie with me."

Three simple words describe her approach: direct, alluring, and, to Joseph, disturbing. Her utter disregard for morality was disturbing. Her brazen approach was disturbing. Her shameless embrace of sensuality was disturbing. Joseph's response was just as abrupt, though he took great care to explain his reasoning: it was the total disrespect for his master and his God that caused his alarm.

Joseph had too much respect for his master to commit such a sin (v. 8). Joseph was, in his master's eyes, much more than a slave. He had been given authority over all that was in his master's house, indicating unconditional trust in Joseph's wisdom and character. To betray such trust would demonstrate shameful disrespect for his master.

Joseph also had too much respect for himself to commit such a sin (v. 9). He told her, "There is none greater in this house than I." That's quite a statement coming from a slave. It indicates a level of character that surpasses a concern for the opinion of others. Joseph knew that an immoral relationship with his master's wife, even if it remained hidden, would destroy that character, making self-respect impossible.

Most importantly, Joseph had too much respect for his God to commit such a sin (v. 9). Everything hinged on his relationship with God. God was the Source of his strength of character. His hope and trust were in God. How could he show disrespect for one who had been so faithful to him?

The temptress, however, was not accustomed to rejection. Joseph's reasoning did nothing to satisfy her sensual desires, and she would not be dissuaded. Her attacks intensified in their manner as well as their frequency. She began to manipulate circumstances so that Joseph would be near and available, and it was becoming more of a challenge for Joseph to avoid her enticements.

That Joseph managed, under those conditions, to remain pure is an amazing testimony to the strength of Joseph's character and the grace of God in his life. There are few things as difficult for a young man to refuse as a beautiful woman who is throwing herself at him. Potiphar's wife was a perfect example of the strange woman described in Proverbs 7:13-20:

> So she caught him, and kissed him, and with an impudent face said unto him, I have peace offerings with me; this day have I payed my vows. Therefore came I forth to meet thee, diligently to seek thy face, and I have found thee. I have decked my bed with coverings of tapestry, with carved works, with fine linen of Egypt. I have perfumed my bed with myrrh, aloes, and cinnamon. Come, let us take our fill of love until the morning: let us solace ourselves with loves. For the goodman is not at home, he is gone a long journey: He hath taken a bag of money with him, and will come home at the day appointed.

It's one thing to resist a single attack. Joseph, however, had to face the same temptation day after day. In normal circumstances, the repetition would weaken the resistance of a man; but Joseph's character had been refined by the challenges he faced in his dysfunctional home. His faith had been strengthened, and his allegiance to God settled: the decision had already been made. It was simply a matter of being true to his previously determined commitment.

Continued denial only made Joseph that much more attractive. Mark Twain once said, "There is a charm about the forbidden that makes it unspeakably desirable."[1] The lure of forbidden fruit was strong; and once more, Potiphar's wife intensified her pursuit.

Because of her authority, it was easy for Potiphar's wife to set the stage for her next attack. She dismissed the other servants so that she would be alone

---

with Joseph when he arrived to perform his duties. Though Scripture doesn't record her preparations in detail, it would be reasonable to assume that she, like the strange woman of Proverbs 7, decked her bed "with coverings of tapestry, with carved works, with fine linen of Egypt," and perfumed her bed "with myrrh, aloes, and cinnamon."

Evil desires, partnered with total disregard for decency and fixed in the heart of an individual exercising authority are, indeed, dangerous. This time, her approach changed. She added a physical element to her request. Instead of simply inviting Joseph to join her in sin, she "caught him by his garment" (Gen. 39:12). She had ignored Joseph's repeated denials; she had scorned his concern for virtue; she had dismissed his wisdom. There was no alternative. She would have her way with Joseph.

Thus far, Joseph had been able to maintain his purity by refusing to be involved. He had kept his distance and stayed busy. Now, the situation has changed. The trap had been sprung, and he found himself firmly in the grasp of his master's wife. The time for reasoning was over. One option remained. He had to get away. So "he left his garment in her hand and fled" (Gen. 39:12).

SUFFERING UNJUSTLY—AGAIN

Once more, Joseph was forced to face the reality that life is not fair. Potiphar's wife was livid. How dare Joseph reject her yet again? Her anger exploding, she called for the men of the house and slandered Joseph with a lie that would seal his fate while protecting her reputation. No one questioned the veracity of her story. After all, she had proof—Joseph's coat. Then she repeated the lie to Potiphar, who promptly condemned Joseph, confining him to prison.

Genesis 39:19 tells us that Potiphar's "wrath was kindled," but we are told nothing about the focus of that wrath. Was he angry at Joseph? If so, why did he allow him to live? Rape, a vicious crime, would certainly warrant death. Perhaps he was angry at the unfortunate consequence of the circumstance that he was forced to confront. Joseph was a valuable servant. Losing him would create a hole that would be difficult to fill.

Could it be that he was angry at his wife? Certainly, he was aware of her character and dismayed by her actions. It is not unlikely that he doubted his wife's story. But he had no choice. Joseph must be punished, so he cast him into "the place where the king's prisoners were bound" (Gen. 39:20). How did Joseph respond to these events? We are not told; but there are a number of possibilities, all of which seem reasonable considering his unfair treatment.

How long must you wait for the fulfillment of a promise or the realization of a dream? Dreams, especially those that come from God, produce wonderful expectations in the heart of a believer, and the events of life become divine steps in the process of reaching that pinnacle. When circumstances, however, hinder progress at every turn, expectations begin to wane. It is natural to begin to doubt.

While resentment is never an acceptable response for a believer, it is far more common than it should be. How many times must he endure unfair treatment? Especially after resisting such direct and sinister temptation. Had he not responded properly? Where was his reward?

Most normal humans would excuse any bitterness Joseph felt toward Potiphar's wife. Not only was she responsible for his unpleasant accommodations, but she had also put an end to his growing prosperity. It would have been easy for Joseph to conclude that she was interfering with God's will for his life. Why was she not punished for her evil deeds?

Discouragement is almost always present when multiple attempts at doing right fail. It is often difficult to maintain a positive spirit when things are going well, especially when sincere effort has been expended to gain that prosperity. When it is suddenly snatched away without cause, disappointment makes it hard to stay positive.

Joseph's attitude, however, was far different. He realized that God was at work in his life. This stop in prison was an indispensable step in God's plan. The Lord would use Joseph's time there to continue to shape his character. Besides, there were some strategic people that Joseph needed to meet, people God would use to move him to the next step on the path to fulfilling his dreams.

Joseph had, for a second time, lost his coat. He also lost his position as overseer in Potiphar's house as well as his freedom. But all was not lost. Joseph retained his integrity and stayed morally pure. Most importantly, his relationship with God remained intact.

DISCUSSION QUESTIONS

1. When Joseph arrived in Egypt, he was immediately taken in by a man named Potiphar, who was a captain of the guard. He was purchased as a slave but soon rose to a position of authority in Potiphar's house. What character qualities did Potiphar observe that led him to trust Joseph with a position of leadership?

2. Potiphar's wife took an interest in Joseph and began a highly focused pursuit of him. How did Joseph respond when he was tempted to compromise his principles by his master's wife? What motivated his response?

3. What was the reaction of Potiphar's wife when Joseph rejected her? Why was she offended?

4. Eventually, Joseph found himself in a hopeless situation. Staying true to his commitment would require personal sacrifice (going to prison). How did Joseph react to this new round of unjust suffering?

5. Scripture tells us that Potiphar's "wrath" was provoked when he heard what had happened. What was the reason for Potiphar's anger? Who was the focus of his wrath?

CHAPTER 5

THE CONFINEMENT

GENESIS 40

BEING IN PRISON IS HARD enough, but it is especially tough when you've been put there under false pretenses. Joseph went to prison because he refused to submit to the immoral solicitation of Potiphar's wife. She was offended because he rejected her. She could not fathom the possibility that Joseph did not find her irresistible. More than that, she could not believe that Joseph would be so bold as to disobey her direct command. That was inexcusable, and Joseph would be forced to pay dearly for what she considered to be a matter of grave disrespect.

Joseph began his stint in prison much like he started his tenure as a slave in Potiphar's house. It was anything but normal. Though he was a prisoner, he didn't act, talk, or look like any other prisoner. There was something unique about his temperament, something that the keeper of the prison noticed immediately. The Lord was merciful to Joseph and gave him favor with the keeper of the prison.

Joseph soon had authority over the other prisoners. He was responsible for their welfare, as well as their activities. And as in Potiphar's house, the Lord made that which he did "to prosper" (Gen. 39:23).

IMPORTANT VISITORS

It is never wise to offend the king of Egypt. Somehow, the king's butler and baker had done so. Whatever they did was serious enough to warrant time in prison. It was the Lord, however, rather than the king, who was actually responsible for their captivity. He had a plan for Joseph, and the butler and baker were key participants.

The butler had a very close relationship with the king. He was, of necessity, the most trusted of the king's servants. It was his responsibility to guarantee the safety and quality of every component of the king's diet. Since the king was still alive and the baker was also in prison, their offense likely pertained to unacceptable quality or taste of the food they presented.

Genesis 40:4 says that the "captain of the guard [Potiphar] charged Joseph with them, and he [Joseph] served them [the butler and the baker)]." Joseph became their personal steward. God, in His sovereignty, placed Joseph in a position that granted him continuous access to a man whose testimony would be crucial to his deliverance.

One of the great scourges of mistreatment is the temptation to feel sorry for yourself. "Why me?" is the immediate response, which is usually followed with "What did I do to deserve this?" In Joseph's case, the answer to the second question would be "Nothing!" Joseph, however, was not one to sit alone in a corner having a pity party. He had learned the value of being productive. His quality of life was determined by choices rather than circumstances. It was that character trait that proved so valuable to his relationship with the officers of the king who were entrusted to his care. Because he was focused on their needs rather than his own, he earned their confidence; and it was easy for them to share their burdens and accept his help.

Both the butler and the baker were alarmed over certain dreams that remained a mystery to them. Dreams had great significance in Egyptian culture, and understanding them provided insight regarding future events. Those uninterpreted dreams caused their distress, which Joseph noticed as he entered their presence one morning. After Joseph assured them of God's interest and ability to provide understanding for them, they began to disclose the details of their dreams.

The butler's dream is revealed in verses nine through eleven. It involved a grapevine with three branches bearing fruit. The grapes were pressed into a cup, which the butler then gave to Pharaoh. Joseph's interpretation brought great joy to the butler: "Yet within three days shall Pharaoh lift up thine head, and restore thee unto thy place: and thou shalt deliver Pharaoh's cup into his hand, after the former manner when thou wast his butler" (v. 13).

Then it was the baker's turn. After hearing the butler's promise of deliverance, he decided to seek Joseph's wisdom as well. The details of his dream are found in verses sixteen through seventeen. He had three baskets on his head, and the top basket contained baked goods for Pharaoh. But the food never made it to Pharaoh's table because the birds feasted on the contents of the basket.

Joseph began his interpretation just as he had with the butler: "Yet within three days shall Pharaoh lift up thy head" (v. 19). Then the interpretation changed, and the butler's heart sank. His head would be "lifted up" all right, but it was to be removed from his body. Then, his headless body would be hung from a tree, where the birds would feast on his flesh.

Both dreams came true, just as Joseph had predicted. The importance of that truth cannot be overstated. It lays a foundation for Pharaoh's future decision to seek Joseph's interpretation of two dreams that were troubling him, dreams that foreshadowed Egypt's greatest challenge and Israel's Divine preservation.

THE IMPACT OF DREAMS

Joseph's journey from the sheepfold in Canaan to the palace in Egypt was charted by dreams. Without them, it would be difficult to understand what God was doing in Joseph's life or how He was doing it. There were dreams to detail God's purpose and plan for Joseph's life, which evoked hatred from his brethren and disbelief from his father. There were dreams by the butler and baker, his fellow prisoners, which God used to deliver Joseph from the grasp of an unjust punishment. Then there were those dreams that troubled Pharaoh, dreams that provided the key to Egypt's future and Israel's survival in the wake of a severe famine.

Joseph's dreams were not unique. In fact, Scripture seems to indicate that they were somewhat common. There are, in Scripture, at least twenty accounts of dreams that had an impact on the lives of individuals. In every case, God used the dream to communicate significant truth that provided guidance to those who were dreaming.

Believers today have the completed canon of Scripture to provide insight concerning God's will and purpose for their lives. There is no extra-biblical truth or new revelation available. That's not to say that God cannot use dreams to inspire believers today. If He does, however, it will be consistent with the teaching of Scripture. Any communication we receive that contradicts the Bible is coming from something other than a Divine source.

JOSEPH'S FORGOTTEN REQUEST

There are those who characterize Joseph's request for the butler's help in verse fourteen as a demonstration of unbelief. Yet it was precisely that request that God used to deliver Joseph from prison (Gen. 41:9-14). Since God directs the movements of men to accomplish His purpose and plan, it is not hard to believe that He actually led Joseph to make the request. Nor is it unreasonable to think that Joseph was trusting God to use the butler's memory. Could God have done it without Joseph's help? Certainly! But there is no reason to malign Joseph's faith because he chose to seek the aid of a human over whom God had sovereign control. Later, when seeking to bring his family to Egypt, Joseph would employ many human methods to accomplish his goal' and God would guide Joseph's steps to make those efforts effective.

Verse fifteen, however, does remind us of Joseph's humanity. For the first time, we see his attitude about the events that brought him, first to Egypt and then to prison. He takes a moment to assure the butler that he is a victim of unjust treatment. He was not a slave, nor had he done anything to deserve imprisonment.

Was Joseph feeling sorry for himself? That question is impossible to answer without knowing Joseph's heart. What we can know is that Joseph was acutely aware of the injustices he suffered; and like most humans, he wanted others to be aware of his innocence.

For two full years, Joseph continued to wait patiently in prison. The butler was so thrilled at the fulfillment of his dream that he could think of little else. He eagerly resumed his duties in the palace and thought no more about the man who correctly interpreted his dream.

Two years is a long time when you are anticipating the arrival of a significant event. During that time, Joseph had the opportunity to feed his offended spirit. He could have sulked and dismayed over the unfair treatment he had received. He could have chosen to abandon his trust in God's plan for his life, but he didn't. How did Joseph deal so effectively with what was surely a severe disappointment?

Joseph understood that suffering is a part of life. As the book of Job puts it, "Yet man is born unto trouble" (Job 5:7). No man has a right to expect that he should live a trouble-free life. We are sinful men living in a sinful world controlled by the prince of evil. The effects of sin produce suffering on every side, and there is no escape. Just as prosperity does not always represent God's blessing, suffering does not always indicate God's judgment. Though Joseph was innocent of the accusation brought by Potiphar's wife, he still had to deal with the natural consequences of sin, as do all men. So what did Joseph do instead of giving in to the temptation of bitterness?

Joseph accepted the circumstances he was facing, though unpleasant, because he was confident of God's presence and purpose in his life. The apostle Paul stated in Philippians 4:11, "I have learned, in whatsoever state I am, therewith to be content." Contentment is not getting what you want but wanting what you have. Joseph decided to want what God allowed to happen to him, understanding that "God meant it unto good" (Gen. 50:20).

Joseph chose to focus on the opportunities for service afforded him rather than the discomfort facing him as a result of his unjust treatment. Life all but stops for some people when things take a turn for the worst. They lose focus, become unproductive, and squander away the most valuable human asset they have: their time. Rather than spend his time regretting his circumstances, Joseph chose to make his life productive. His service to the other prisoners was an encouragement to them; but far more importantly, it gave Joseph purpose in the midst of his trial.

It would have been easy for Joseph to question the wisdom of embracing a dream that seemed so distant. He could have chosen to yield to the temptation to live as others do, gaining temporal fulfillment by gratifying fleshly desires. Why put forth the effort to embrace eternal values when doing so provided no reward?

But Joseph's attitude was not determined by feelings. He was committed to staying true to his God for the duration. His faith allowed him to see beyond the confinement of the prison wall, beyond the temporary discomfort of his present circumstances. He knew that his God was in control, so he waited patiently for deliverance.

DISCUSSION QUESTIONS

1. Joseph found himself having to adjust to being in prison, though he did nothing wrong. Somehow he was able to maintain a positive attitude. Who was responsible for Joseph's prosperity while a prisoner? What did that prosperity look like?

2. If we consider the circumstances Joseph faced and observe the consequences of his response to the temptation he dealt with, we have to conclude that there was more than one person responsible for his imprisonment. What individuals were involved in the decision, and how did each contribute to Joseph's confinement? What did Joseph's faith indicate about who he thought was responsible?

3. Both the butler and the baker had dreams that Joseph was able to interpret for them while they were together. How was Joseph able to help them? Who was responsible for the interpretation? Why were those dreams important to Joseph's future?

4. Joseph spent two long years in prison waiting for deliverance. How did Joseph deal with circumstances that were, by human standards, severely unfair?

5. In every situation we face, we have to make a choice about who or what is going to control our response. What choice did Joseph make?

CHAPTER 6
THE PROMOTION

GENESIS 41

IT IS NEVER WISE TO offend the king of Egypt, and Joseph wasn't about to make that mistake. The king had had two dreams, neither of which he understood. Consequently, "his spirit was troubled; and he sent and called for all the magicians of Egypt, and all the wise men thereof: and Pharaoh told them his dream; but there was none that could interpret them unto Pharaoh" (Gen. 41:8).

Pharaoh's dreams caused him great distress. He understood that they were more than the usual random, insignificant night visions. Yet he was baffled by their meaning, troubled by the possibility that they foretold dreadful events, and unable to dismiss them from his mind. He remained unenlightened, even after enlisting the help of the most learned men in his kingdom.

When the butler heard about Pharaoh's dilemma, his memory returned; and he told the king of his experience with the unusual man with whom he had shared a cell while in prison, who had the ability to interpret dreams. Finally, a turning point for Joseph begins: "Then Pharaoh sent and called Joseph" (v. 14).

At no time in Joseph's life was the Sovereign handiwork of God more obvious. God had given dreams to Joseph when he was seventeen years old, revealing Joseph's future. He had given dreams to the butler and the baker to prepare the way for Joseph's deliverance from prison. Now He gave dreams to Pharaoh to complete the process. Then God prodded the butler to remember the promise he had made to Joseph.

AN AUDIENCE WITH THE KING

Joseph took care to avoid offending Pharaoh. Egyptian culture placed a great deal of emphasis on cleanliness and hygiene; therefore, visible hair was almost nonexistent among Egyptian men. Beards, however, were the norm for men in Israel. To avoid the possibility of offense, Joseph took time before his appointment with Pharaoh to shave, wash, and change his clothes.

When Joseph arrived at the palace, the king was waiting for him. Joseph met a man carrying a heavy burden. Pharaoh was aware of the significance of his dreams, and he was most anxious to learn their meaning. He wasted little time with pleasantries: "I have dreamed a dream, and there is none that can interpret it: and I have heard say of thee, that thou canst understand a dream to interpret it" (Gen. 41:15).

While Joseph was rightly concerned about the danger of offending Pharaoh, he was more concerned about offending God. Joseph's integrity constrained his answer. He dared not take credit for what God was about to do, nor would he yield to the temptation to feign superiority over the wise men of Egypt. Instead, Joseph's response was a wonderful testimony to the wisdom, grace, and power of his God. He assured Pharaoh that the interpretation would not come from his human wisdom or ability. God would reveal his plan for Egypt, a revelation that would "give Pharaoh an answer of peace" (Gen. 41:16).

PHARAOH'S DREAMS

Pharaoh had had two dreams. The first revealed seven fat kine (cows) followed by seven very lean kine who then consumed the fat kine. The second was a mirror image of the first, except that the message was conveyed by ears of corn rather than cattle. In either case, the first group consumed the second, yet they were no better off for having done so.

Two elements provided essential guidance as Joseph explained Pharaoh's dreams. First, the two dreams were actually one. God had doubled Pharaoh's dreams to emphasize their importance. The coming events were "established by God" (v. 32). Second, Joseph revealed the prophetic significance of the dreams. God was being gracious to Pharaoh, giving him insight into His plans for Egypt. Three times, Joseph reminded the king that these were things that God was "about to do" (vs. 25, 28, 32).

Egypt was to enjoy seven years of abundance, marked by pastures filled with healthy cattle and fields overflowing with grain. The next seven years would produce a famine so severe that the years of plenty would be quickly forgotten. The meaning was clear. The coming events were "established by God" (v. 32).

God's grace was guiding Joseph as he provided wisdom for Pharaoh. Knowing that the famine was coming was challenging enough, but preparing to deal with it was intimidating. Nevertheless, God had a plan, and He gave Joseph the particulars: Pharaoh needed to find a man he could trust, someone with wisdom and discretion, to guide the nation through the difficult years ahead. As the senior administrator of the program, he would appoint officers who would be responsible for collecting a fifth of all that was produced throughout the land for the seven years of plenty. That food, collected and stored during those years of prosperity, would be the source of their provision during the years of famine.

It didn't take Pharaoh long to conclude that Joseph's wisdom and discernment were no fluke. Besides, those were not the only qualities Joseph possessed that drew him to Pharaoh. In verse thirty-eight, Pharaoh poses a question to his servants: "Can we find such a one as this is, a man in whom the Spirit of God is?" Joseph had been very conscientious about deflecting credit from himself to his God, and Pharaoh acknowledged as much when he said to Joseph, "Forasmuch as God hath shewed thee all this, there is none so discreet and wise as thou art: Thou shalt be over my house, and according unto thy word shall all my people be ruled: only in the throne will I be greater than thou" (Gen. 41:39-40).

Pharaoh came to the logical conclusion that Joseph was a Divine messenger sent to provide the wisdom necessary to prepare them for the coming famine. Therefore, it only made sense to empower Joseph to carry out the plan God had given him. No one else was competent to fill the position, least of all the unskilled wise men of Egypt.

Joseph's appointment as senior administrator of Pharaoh's household provided substantial benefits. Joseph became second in authority over all of Egypt. Pharaoh's ring was placed on his finger, and people were commanded to "bow the knee" (v. 43) in reverence when his chariot passed by. His name was changed along with his wardrobe, and when he married "Asenath the daughter of Potipherah priest of On" (v. 45), he became a highly respected citizen of Egypt.

Scripture reveals little about Joseph's emotional reaction to his promotion. What was his immediate response? It would have been natural for him to feel a bit of vindication at finally being promoted. But Joseph's reactions have been consistently unnatural. He never seemed to resent the unpleasant afflictions he was forced to bear. He never hesitated to embrace the unexpected duties that were thrust upon him. There was no evidence of a vengeful spirit or bitter attitude.

I'm sure that Potiphar and his wife were keenly interested in Joseph's promotion. How would he choose to exercise his power? Would he seek to retaliate against those who had mistreated him? If so, they would have been in grave danger. But there is no indication of such a response. Scripture states simply that "Joseph went out over all the land of Egypt" (v. 45). In other words, Joseph did exactly what he was expected to do, calmly, carefully, and deliberately discharging his newly assumed responsibilities.

It had been thirteen years since Joseph was sold by his brothers to the Midianite merchantmen. He endured the hardship of unjust enslavement, conquered the carnal enticement of Potiphar's wife, and survived more than two full years of fraudulent imprisonment. His dreams were despised by his jealous brothers. His coat of many colors was stolen and used to deceive his father into thinking he was dead. Later, his outer garment, left in the hands of his master's wife, was used falsely to provoke his incarceration. Yet Joseph's heart never wavered. He remained true to his God and maintained his integrity.

Joseph was now thirty years old. He had traveled a rocky road from a pit to a palace. His father's coat of many colors was gone, and in its place was a royal wardrobe of fine linen. His neck and hands were graced with gold, rather than the grime of the pasture. Instead of obeying orders, he issued them; and no one ridiculed his opinions. He had, indeed, come a long way. God had given him a position of great honor and glory. But the primary objective of Joseph's life was not his exaltation. It was the salvation of his family, the preservation of a nation, and the provision of a redeemer. Joseph's exaltation was but one essential step in the process, and Joseph's story was just beginning.

A SEASON OF PLENTY

For the next seven years, Egypt enjoyed bumper crops in every field. Genesis 41:47 states that "the earth brought forth by handfuls." So great was the harvest that Joseph was unable to track it accurately. Little by little, the stockpiles grew; and careful plans were carried out to prepare for the coming famine. Events were unfolding exactly as God had revealed.

In later years, Joseph's father would refer to him as "a fruitful bough, even a fruitful bough by a well; whose branches run over the wall" (Gen. 49:22). During those years of plenty, Joseph's fruitfulness was manifested in the birth of two sons: "And Joseph called the name of the firstborn Manasseh: For God, said he, hath made me forget all my toil, and all my father's house. And the name of the second called he Ephraim: For God hath caused me to be fruitful in the land of my affliction" (Gen. 41:51-52).

What a wonderful demonstration of Joseph's attitude toward the circumstances that had shaped his life thus far: "God has made me to forget my affliction, and God has made me fruitful in the midst of that affliction."

A SEASON OF POVERTY

As the time of abundance came to an end, the seven years of famine began, just as God had promised. The poverty produced by the famine affected all lands, with one exception, facilitated by God's grace and Joseph's obedience: "in all the land of Egypt there was bread" (Gen. 41:54).

Now, it was time for Joseph to demonstrate the wisdom, power, and compassion of his God. Because of Joseph's faithfulness to execute God's perfect plan, the storehouses were full of grain; there was enough to meet the needs of every nation. Joseph "opened all the storehouses" and began selling the grain to those in need, "and all countries came into Egypt to Joseph to buy corn" (Gen. 41:57).

DISCUSSION QUESTIONS

1. After two years in prison, Joseph was summoned to an audience with the king of Egypt. He was called because Pharaoh was looking for someone—anyone who could interpret two very alarming dreams that he had—and the butler remembered Joseph's ability to interpret dreams. How did Joseph prepare for the meeting? How did Joseph respond to Pharaoh's confidence in his ability to interpret dreams?

2. Dreams played a huge role in Joseph's journey. What were those dreams, and how did God use them to order Joseph's steps?

3. After meeting with Joseph and learning the meaning of his dreams, Pharaoh came to a conclusion about who should provide leadership for the coming challenge. What influenced Pharaoh's decision to appoint Joseph as governor of Egypt?

4. What benefits did Joseph receive with that appointment?

5. Did Joseph's attitude change when he became governor? What influence, if any, did the appointment have on Joseph's faith in God?

CHAPTER 7

THE FAMINE: PART ONE

GENESIS 42

JACOB AND HIS SONS WERE in great anguish. The famine had been growing progressively worse, and there was no end in sight. If they were unable to obtain food soon, they would all die. Individuals deal with hardship in different ways, and their response is always a reflection of their character mitigated by their resources. Poor character combined with meager assets will usually cause panic, while those with strong character always seem to find a way to survive no matter their level of poverty. Jacob's sons were wealthy, but their character was weak. That combination is a breeding ground for corruption.

Though food was available in Egypt and Jacob had the resources to purchase it, his sons showed no interest in taking advantage of that opportunity. Instead of going to purchase food, they gathered to sulk over their misfortune. It wasn't until Jacob reprimanded them for their indolence and ordered them to go that they journeyed to Egypt to buy food. All except one made the trip. Benjamin, Joseph's younger brother, stayed home. Jacob was unwilling to risk his safety, "lest peradventure mischief befall him" (Gen. 42:4).

A PROPHESY FULFILLED

Joseph's brothers had no idea what God had planned for them. They knew they were facing a long journey: two hundred miles. They knew that they were to purchase grain for their family, a weighty responsibility. They knew that their father was skeptical of their ability or willingness to protect their youngest brother, Benjamin. They did not know that they would bow before their bartered brother, nor did they know that their flimsy integrity would be sorely tested many times.

When the delegation arrived, they were ushered into the presence of the governor of Egypt, a man of imposing dignity and absolute authority, a man who would determine their future. It is only reasonable to assume that they were intimidated. Like every delegation that had come to meet with Joseph, they "bowed down themselves before him with their faces to the earth" (Gen. 42:6). There was no way for them to know that the man who held their survival in his hands, the man at whose feet they were bowing, was their hated brother, Joseph.

While Joseph had no trouble recognizing his brethren, he intentionally thwarted their ability to identify him, making himself "strange" to them. His age, appearance, accent, and authority would have made it difficult to identify the man in front of the as their younger brother.

Joseph was only seventeen years old when his brothers last saw him, and the picture emblazoned on their memory was the face of a young man in agony over the unjust treatment they were dishing out. Joseph was now almost forty, and he was certainly not in distress. While age alone was not enough to dampen their ability to recognize the man before whom they stood, it certainly played a part.

Joseph had taken on the appearance of an Egyptian. He had an Egyptian name and an Egyptian wife. He was clean-shaven and wore the garb of the second-ranking official in Egypt. Pharaoh's ring adorned Joseph's hand, giving him authority over all but Pharaoh himself.

Joseph had become intensely entwined with Egyptian culture. He lived as an Egyptian, acted like an Egyptian, and spoke their language. Even if the hindrances listed above didn't exist, Joseph's brothers would have been hard-pressed to believe that the young man they sold into slavery was now the governor of Egypt. That idea would have been preposterous.

What started with spontaneous intimidation soon progressed to focused interrogation. Joseph knew who they were and why they came, yet he chose to conceal his identity. He "spake roughly unto them" (v. 7) and accused them of espionage. It would not have been unusual for such an incident to occur. Spies often came to Egypt intending to learn their military weaknesses ("nakedness of the land").

There can be no doubt that Joseph felt some satisfaction from the shift in positions that had occurred. Verse nine states that "Joseph remembered the dreams which he dreamed of them." He was no longer the hated younger brother dealing with the unfair treatment of older, contemptuous siblings. His older brothers had, indeed, bowed before him. He was in control.

DEALING WITH SIN

It had been more than twenty years since Joseph had last seen his brethren, but the circumstances leading to their separation were still crystal clear in his mind. The feelings of rejection, loneliness, and utter helplessness that accompanied his time in the pit had long since been overcome; but to forget them would have required far greater discipline than possessed by any mortal.

Some insist that Joseph harbored no lingering bitterness toward his brethren, no hint of anger that would provoke him to seek or demand revenge. Even so, Joseph, knowing who they were and why they came, chose to accuse them falsely. While it is impossible to know Joseph's motive in making the accusation, we do know that the accusation came immediately after remembering his dreams and that Joseph displayed no compassion when his siblings insisted that their mission was limited to purchasing food. After repeating the charge four times, Joseph confined them to a cell.

Perhaps Joseph's harsh treatment was deliberately calculated to compel his brothers to acknowledge their sin. For three days, they agonized, pondering their circumstances, rehearsing their misdeeds, and trying to devise a solution to their dilemma. They were facing certain death unless they could produce their youngest brother, and convincing their aged father to entrust Benjamin to their care would be virtually impossible.

Joseph's first decree permitted one of the brothers to return to Canaan to fetch Benjamin. The other nine were to be held in prison until Benjamin returned. After three days, Joseph revealed a new plan. His previous instructions had been reversed: one brother would remain in prison while the other nine went to get their younger brother. Failure to return with Benjamin would result in death.

Three days in prison stirred their lifeless consciences. Joseph's brethren found themselves agonizing over their misfortune, and they were quick to acknowledge the cause: "We are verily guilty concerning our brother, in that we saw the anguish of his soul, when he besought us, and we would not hear; therefore is this distress come upon us" (Gen. 42:21).

Guilt has a way of transforming perceptions, and the sons of Jacob were surely seeing things differently. Each of them willingly took responsibility for his part in the ruthless treatment of their younger brother. They forgot about the unfair favoritism shown toward Joseph by their father. There was no mention of Joseph's coat of many colors or his offensive dreams of supremacy. Instead, they remembered the "anguish of his soul" and their cruel indifference to his pleas for mercy. Now, they were the ones needing mercy; and unlike Joseph, their treatment was justified.

Reuben, however, was not prepared to accept responsibility. He had encouraged his brethren not to harm Joseph, convincing them to delay their plans briefly to give him an opportunity to rescue his younger brother. His efforts were, however, unsuccessful, so he reminded them that they alone were guilty of their brother's blood.

What they couldn't know was that Joseph heard and understood every word they said. As Joseph listened to their conversation, his emotions were stirred' and he lost his composure—so much so that he had to leave their presence to recover. When he returned, he selected the brother who would be retained in Egypt until they returned with Benjamin. Reuben was the oldest and would have been the likely choice, but Reuben's words had confirmed his innocence. Instead, Joseph chose Simeon, the second oldest, and "bound him before their eyes" (v. 24).

RETURNING HOME

Though Joseph released his brothers to return home, he wasn't done applying pressure. At Joseph's command, each brother's money was returned to his sack, along with adequate provisions for his journey. When the men reached their stopping point for the night, one of them opened his sack to get food for his donkey and found his money. The discovery caused fear, and their guilt continued to build. They were certain that God was avenging their treatment of Joseph, whom they assumed was dead.

When they reached their father's house, things got worse. What should have been a time of rejoicing turned to abject despair. Jacob's sons told their father, in precise detail, everything that had happened to them in Egypt.

Jacob, who had spent more than twenty years grieving over the death of his son Joseph, now added Simeon to his list of sorrows; and the idea that Benjamin should return with them to Egypt was unthinkable. Jacob's assertion that "all these things are against me" (v. 36) surely added to their guilt. It was, after all, their choice to sell Joseph to the Midianites. They were the ones who bloodied Joseph's coat of many colors and allowed their father to assume he was dead. Jacob's grief was so severe that he refused to consider any plan that put the life of Benjamin at risk. Verse thirty-eight suggests that he would rather let his family starve than risk harm to his youngest son. And they alone were responsible.

DISCUSSION QUESTIONS

1. Chapter forty-two of the book of Genesis begins with Jacob observing the idleness of his sons in the midst of a frightful famine. When Jacob learned that there was corn available in Egypt, he sent his sons (all but Benjamin) to purchase grain. Why did Jacob insist that Benjamin stay home?

2. When Jacob's sons arrived in Egypt, they presented themselves before the governor, who was responsible for distributing the food. Then, in a partial fulfillment of Joseph's first dream (Benjamin was not with them), they bowed before him. Why were they unable to recognize their younger brother, Joseph?

3. How did Joseph's brethren respond when accused of being spies?

4. After he held them for three days in custody, Joseph agreed to keep Simeon in jail and allow the rest of them to return home with their grain, with one stipulation: they must bring their youngest brother with them when they return. How did Joseph's brothers respond when hearing that news? What does their conversation reveal about their claim of innocence?

5. Joseph's brothers were unaware that Joseph understood their conversation. What did Joseph learn about the circumstances surrounding his betrayal by his brothers? How did it affect him?

6. How did Joseph's brothers react to finding the money they took to purchase food restored in their sacks?

7. What was Jacob's response when Simeon did not return and upon learning that Benjamin would have to accompany them if they needed to go again?

CHAPTER 8

THE FAMINE: PART TWO

GENESIS 43

THOUGH WE ARE NOT TOLD how long it took Jacob's family to consume the corn they obtained in Egypt, we can confidently assume that it happened much too quickly. Once again, Jacob found himself in need of provisions to survive; so he instructed his sons to "Go again, buy us a little food" (Gen. 43:2).

Hearing their father suggest so calmly that they should return to Egypt must have caused Jacob's sons to bristle with fear. Judah took the lead in challenging his father's plan, reminding him that they had been warned by the governor not to return without their younger brother. He then made it clear that without Benjamin, they would not be returning to Egypt. After dealing with Jacob's suggestion that their guilt was greater because they had been careless enough to tell the Egyptian master that they had a younger brother, Judah boldly proposed a solution to the problem.

Benjamin must return with them to Egypt—there was no other option. If they returned to Egypt without him, they would surely die. If they did not return to Egypt to purchase grain, they were going to die. Their only hope was to take Benjamin with them.

Judah would take responsibility for Benjamin. Reuben, Jacob's firstborn, had already addressed the issue of security for Benjamin if they made the return trip, offering his sons in exchange for Benjamin's safety, an offer which Jacob adamantly refused. Judah's promise was much more personal; he alone would "bear the blame forever" (v. 9) if Benjamin did not return.

Jacob finally acknowledged the severity of their crisis and accepted the potential consequences. His sons must return to Egypt with Benjamin. Even so, they would take extreme measures to soften any culpability from the last trip. They took gifts for the governor along with double payment to cover the cost of their previous purchase.

JACOB'S UNBELIEF

Faith requires moving forward without a clear understanding of the outcome. It requires unconditional trust in the one who controls the outcome of all things. It requires believing that your God cares about what happens to you while knowing that He will keep his promises. Yet Jacob's words convey no such confidence. Instead, we find him evaluating things from a purely emotional perspective.

Though Jacob agreed to allow Benjamin to return to Egypt, he did so with a solemn dread that speaks volumes about his lack of trust in God. He considers the possibility that the governor may release Simeon when he sees Benjamin but demonstrates little optimism for such an outcome. He appears to be solemnly resolved to spend the rest of his life mourning the loss of his youngest sons.

Jacob's entire life had been characterized by a lack of faith. He chose to walk by sight rather than faith, seeking to "help" God by first stealing his brother's birthright, then his blessing. He fathered children by Bilhah, Rachel's handmade, to compensate for the children Rachel was unable to bear. He deceived Laban, his uncle and employer, by devising a scheme that made sure that his share of the cattle and sheep were produced by the healthy stock rather than those that were feeble. In this case, however, Jacob had no power to manipulate the outcome; and he was unsure of God's desire or willingness to protect Benjamin. That doubt destroyed Jacob's hope and left him in great despair.

Guilt is a powerful emotion. It creates regret mixed with fear in the heart of an individual who refuses to acknowledge his sin. Every unpleasant circumstance that occurs becomes a possible punishment for unreconciled deeds, and every unexpected event creates severe anxiety. Jacob's words may have been contrived to stimulate guilt in the hearts of his sons. They certainly did not offer encouragement. He challenged them regarding their foolishness in revealing the existence of their younger brother to the governor, suggesting that they did it maliciously to cause their father pain. He identified Benjamin as "their brother" rather than "his son," perhaps seeking to emphasize their responsibility for him. Finally, after offering an appeal for God's mercy, he concedes that he may be forced to accept the loss of his children. The implication to his sons was that such a result would be their fault.

The second trip must have seemed much longer than the first. Though the distance was the same, the circumstances had become much more dire. The first trip had one purpose: to procure food for the family. The second trip required a more measured approach. What answer would they provide if they were accused of taking their initial supply of grain without paying for it? Would they be successful in their attempt to secure the release of their brother Simeon? What would they do if the governor chose to keep their youngest brother, Benjamin? We can be sure that those questions added a much greater burden than the supplies they carried for their journey.

A SECOND MEETING WITH THE GOVERNOR

When Jacob's sons arrived in Egypt the second time, they again stood before their younger brother, Joseph. Joseph's second meeting with his brothers was very different from the first. While his brothers were pondering their fate, Joseph was dealing with his own emotional roller coaster. Joseph's first encounter with his brothers was unexpected, the second anticipated.

The first encounter stirred Joseph's memory; the second re-introduced him to his younger brother. The first encounter led to pointed interrogation, the second to a celebration. And with each new order from the governor, Joseph's brothers grew more uneasy.

Seeing his younger brother must have been difficult for Joseph. Verse sixteen reveals that Joseph's attention was focused on Benjamin. Joseph must have wondered how Benjamin had fared in his relationship with his older brothers. After the presumed death of Joseph, Benjamin would have inherited the status of "favored son" with his father, along with the intense hatred of his brothers. Had Benjamin been treated as harshly as was Joseph?

Joseph did not tarry to talk with his brothers when they arrived but immediately gave orders that they were to dine with him at noon and left them with the ruler of his house. He did not even speak to his brothers. Perhaps he did not trust his emotions. At the very least, he did not feel comfortable to reveal his identity to them. There were more steps that had to be accomplished before that could happen.

Meanwhile, Joseph's brothers were dealing with their own emotional meltdown. Fear and guilt mixed with a plan to make amends for previous offenses dominated their thinking, and being brought directly into Joseph's house did little to dispel their torment. They were sure that the governor was determined to ensnare them, even suggesting that the money that was returned in their sacks was the trapping device. Bondage was the inevitable consequence. Verses twenty through twenty-two record the first of two passionate attempts to convey their innocence. Their defense contained four elements, and each statement was an attempt to provide an answer for a wrong that they did not do.

"O sir, we came indeed down at the first time to buy food" (Gen. 43:10) was their first line of defense. There was no motive other than their hunger, and the only place to get food was Egypt. Next, they explained, "And it came to pass, when we came to the inn, that we opened our sacks, and behold, every man's money was in the mouth of his sack, our money in full weight: and we have brought it again in our hand" (Gen. 43:21). They were shocked to find the money they gave to the steward back in their sacks and they are returning that money in full. They assured the governor of their good intentions, saying, "And other money we have brought down in our hands to buy food:" (Gen. 43:22a). Finally, they restated their innocence: "We cannot tell who put our money in our sacks" (Gen. 23:22b).

They offered this explanation not because they had been accused but because of their personal guilt. Joseph's steward in no way implied that they were guilty of having done any wrong. Instead, he ignores their plea and offers a blatantly deceitful explanation for how the money was returned to their sacks. He made two statements that were untrue. He told them that God had given them "treasure" in their sacks. While God was certainly in control of the events that transpired on the previous trip, the steward (at Joseph's command) rather than God was responsible for the return of the money. Then he said to them, "I had your money" (v. 23), which was another mistruth. Then he returned their brother Simeon to them.

The steps which followed must have seemed very strange to them. First, the steward brought them into the house of the governor, the same man who had previously accused them of being spies. He gave them water to drink and cared for their donkeys while allowing them to wash their feet. Then they learned that they were going to dine with the governor. We are not told what they were thinking at this time, but we can be sure that their anxiety was growing. Was this an additional step in the governor's plan to entrap them? At what point would they be arrested and placed in the servant's quarters? Remember that their thoughts are still being controlled by their guilt. While we don't know how long, we do know that Joseph did not return home for a period of time, giving them ample opportunity to exaggerate their unpleasant expectations.

A DREAM FULFILLED AND A HEART OVERWHELMED

When Joseph did get home, the brothers did two things. They presented the governor with the gift they had prepared and then bowed before him. Only this time, Benjamin was with them; and Simeon had been returned to their company. All eleven of his brothers were there, and all eleven of them bowed before their brother Joseph. After asking questions about the health of his father, Joseph turned his attention to his younger, full-blooded brother Benjamin, whom he had not seen in more than twenty years. He made one statement to Benjamin, conveying a personal desire that God would show him good favor, and then excused himself.

It's hard to imagine the flood of emotions that Joseph must have experienced at that moment. Not only had his brothers, those who sold him into slavery, bowed at his feet, but he would soon be reunited with the other son of his mother, Benjamin. When an unexpected yet eagerly awaited reunion finally occurs, the tears need no help to flood the eyes. Gratitude and joy naturally fill the heart, and attempting to hide that kind of emotion is futile. Joseph was not yet ready to reveal his identity to his brothers, so it was necessary for him to find a place where he could settle his emotions and regain his composure. When Joseph returned, he was once again the calm, confident, self-composed ruler to whom they had become accustomed.

The next sequence of events had to disconcert the sons of Jacob. Joseph gave one simple command—"Set on bread"—and the steward went to work. They placed a table at the head where Joseph would eat. Then, they prepared a separate place for the Egyptians to eat. Finally, they set up another table where the Hebrews would eat. Thus far, there would be no questions because they would have understood the cultural taboo associated with Hebrews and Egyptians intermingling. Then things began to get strange. They seated Joseph's brothers at the table according to their birth order, and the men began to wonder what was going on. They then set generous servings of delicious food before each man, and Benjamin was the last of the brothers to receive his food. They first brought him a serving equal to what his brothers received. Then they brought him a second equal portion. Then a third, a fourth, and a fifth.

When the evening was over and the brothers retreated to their sleeping quarters, they had much to ponder. Several reasonable questions came to mind: Why were they being treated so kindly after having been initially accused as spies? How did the steward know the order of their birth? Why did Benjamin receive so much more food than the others? What was awaiting them in the morning?

While we cannot know all that they were thinking, it's not hard to imagine that they did not sleep well. Although they had been treated very kindly, they had not yet been released to return home. Their guilt, which had not been resolved, was still gnawing at them, and we can be sure that their discussions were filled with unforeseen possibilities of severe retribution yet to come. They would not have long to wait. Their gut-wrenching shame and remorse would spill out uncontrollably shortly after they started for home the next morning.

DISCUSSION QUESTIONS

1. After some time, the corn ran out; and Jacob realized that his sons would need to make a return trip to Egypt. How did Jacob's sons react to his demand that they go back and face the governor of Egypt a second time without their brother Benjamin?

2. Who finally spoke up, telling their father that they would only return to Egypt if Benjamin went with them? How did Jacob react to their reply? Did Jacob's response indicate a strong level of trust in his God?

3. When they got to Egypt, it was Joseph's steward who met them rather than Joseph Why did Joseph's brothers work so hard to declare their innocence regarding the money they found in their sacks, even though they had not been accused of a crime?

4. How was Joseph's second meeting with his brothers different from the first? What was Joseph's reaction when he saw his brother Benjamin?

5. At the end of verse thirty-three, we read that "the men marveled one at another." What does that statement mean, and why did it happen?

CHAPTER 9

THE CONFESSION

GENESIS 44

GUILT IS A HARD TASKMASTER, making slaves of its victims. Hope for relief is nonexistent. Every bad thing that happens is viewed as possible punishment for the offense committed, and good things that happen cannot be fully enjoyed because of the very real awareness that nothing good is deserved. Life is tedious at best and tortuous at worst as the guilty one wonders and waits for the reckoning to come.

Dealing with guilt is a process that moves through four stages:

1. Guilt is established by corruption. Authentic guilt is not the result of simply making a mistake. Sometimes, we choose to call it guilt when we have done something unintentional that causes pain or creates hardship for someone else. I believe a better word for that occasion is remorse, a sorrow of heart for having accidentally adversely affected the life of someone else. Remorse usually results in an immediate, genuine apology accompanied by an attempt to make amends. Authentic guilt is established (brought about or set in motion) by a pre-meditated decision to do something wrong. There is no desire or effort to rectify the wrong committed.

2.   Guilt is exacerbated by concealment. The first goal of an offender after his crime is always to find a way to cover it up. Joseph's brothers covered their sin by presenting Joseph's coat to their father, covered in blood. The obvious problem is that once you make that first attempt to cover your sin, you realize that now you have two sins to cover rather than one, and the process never stops. To make things worse, the hiding places become harder to find; and the guilt intensifies.

3.   Guilt is exposed by conviction. At some point, the hiding places become non-existent. Joseph's brothers had, to this point, been successful in deceiving their father about the death of their younger brother. They had lived for twenty years with the knowledge of what they had done buried inside their hearts. But it wasn't buried so deep that they were able to forget it. They had already discussed it once when Joseph had accused them of being spies (Gen. 42:17-21). Every time they were accused by an outsider for whatever offense they may or may not have committed, they were also accused again by their own consciences for what they knew they had done. That is where we find the sons of Jacob as they begin their journey home with all of their brothers (including Simeon and Benjamin) along with the grain that was the objective of the trip.

4.   Guilt is eliminated by confession. Confession is more than admitting that you have done wrong. It is more than being sorry for what you have done (remorse). It is the gut-wrenching awareness that you must find relief from the burden you are carrying, and you do not care who learns of your sin or the price you must pay to achieve that goal. The desire to conceal the sin is gone along with any attempt to justify what you have done. All efforts of defense have been abandoned, and you realize that

the only hope you have is the mercy of the one whom you have offended. At that point, conviction has done its work.

ONE FINAL TEST

When Judah and his brothers awoke the next morning, they found their sacks stuffed with grain and their carts loaded. Once the sun began to appear, they were sent on their way. Leaving the city behind as they departed from Egypt must have been quite a relief. They had achieved every one of their goals. They purchased the grain they needed, retrieved Simeon from his bondage, secured the safety of Benjamin, and were now on their way back to Canaan. It would be a long but pleasant journey home.

Joseph, however, had one last surprise. He decided to tighten the screws just a bit more, just enough to bring them to a place of utter dismay. He had instructed his steward to place a very special silver cup in the mouth of Benjamin's sack, then chase them down and accuse them of stealing the cup and rewarding "evil for good" (Gen. 44:4).

Joseph's brothers were absolutely stunned when the steward arrived and made the accusation. Once again, they were being accused unjustly. They were not spies! They did not have the silver cup! They were not thieves! They were so bold in their response and so certain of their innocence that they made a very serious but ill-advised pledge: "With whomsoever of thy servants it be found, both let him die, and we also will be my lord's bondmen" (Gen. 44:9).

The steward accepted their pledge but with a significant change: only the one in whose sack the cup was found would become his servant. The rest of them would go free (v. 10). Then, with the agreement of all the brothers, the search began. The search started with Judah's sack and continued until they got to Benjamin's sack. At that point, Joseph's brothers had to be feeling that their innocence was finally being rewarded. There was no possibility that the cup would be found in Benjamin's sack. Just a few more minutes and they could resume their journey.

Yet Judah and his brothers were not innocent. To be sure, they did not steal the silver cup; but they were not innocent. Lacking genuine confession, guilt never goes away; and conviction continued its work, reminding them, accusing them of the unconfessed deed that remained concealed in their hearts. When the cup was discovered in Benjamin's sack, we can be sure it was their sin against their brother Joseph that appeared before them in all of its disgust; and at that point, there was no escape. They rent their clothes and made their way back to the home of the governor of Egypt.

Did they have an opportunity to talk on the return trip? Did they begin to wonder why their younger brother Benjamin seemed to be the focus of so much attention? First, the ruler asked them to identify Benjamin and then suddenly left. The next time they saw the ruler was at the dinner, and Benjamin received five times more food than the rest of them. How did the silver cup get into Benjamin's sack? And why were they so foolish as to make a pledge that would, at the very least, result in Benjamin becoming the servant of the steward?

All of them were obviously in distress, but it was one man who carried the greatest burden. Judah had made himself surety for his youngest brother. His promise to his father was strong and clear: "I will be surety for him; of my hand shalt thou require him: if I bring him not unto thee, and set him before thee, then let me bear the blame for ever" (Gen. 43:9).

Therefore, it is no surprise that when they arrived back at Joseph's house and heard, once again, the false accusation regarding the silver cup that it was Judah who spoke up: "What shall we say unto my lord? what shall we speak? or how shall we clear ourselves? God hath found out the iniquity of thy servants: behold, we are my lord's servants, both we, and he also with whom the cup is found" (Gen. 44:16).

Judah's confession was clear, concise, and complete. There was no attempt to justify, excuse, or explain their sin. His words made it clear that they had no defense, and they were ready to accept whatever punishment was to come.

The goal was freedom from the constant pressure of hiding their sin. They wanted to be rid of their guilt.

Joseph, however, had one final bit of pressure to apply. The consequence of their sin was the very thing that they could not imagine happening, the one thing that was absolutely unacceptable. The ten oldest brothers were free to go, but Benjamin would remain in Egypt with Joseph. Joseph was casually sending them home without their younger brother.

What follows is one of the most poignant, gut-wrenching pleas found anywhere in Scripture. Judah absolutely fell apart, his emotions unchecked as he sought to change the mind of the man standing before him. He began by reminding Joseph of the circumstances which led them to this point. He recalled Joseph's insistence that Benjamin accompany them on their return trip and related their father's agony over the prospect of letting him go. He explained that Benjamin was the surviving son of two sons who were born to their father later in life and that the other son was presumed to have been "torn in pieces." Returning without Benjamin would surely cause the death of their father. Judah's final revelation was that he had personally guaranteed the safe return of Benjamin to his father. If his younger brother did not return home with him, he alone would "bear the blame to [his] father forever" (Gen. 43:9). Judah wrapped up his appeal by offering himself as a servant in Joseph's house in the place of his brother Benjamin.

Judah's outburst was the result of more than twenty years of guilt building in the hearts of a group of men who had tragically wronged their younger brother. The last time they saw Joseph, he had been loaded onto a wagon and was on his way to Egypt. In their minds, they had dashed his dreams, humbled his spirit, and ridden themselves of a man that they hated, so much so that they "could not speak peaceably unto him" (Gen. 37:4). While they thought they were putting an end to a very unpleasant episode in their lives, they were also beginning a new, far more painful experience that would change them dramatically.

For more than twenty years, Judah and his brothers watched the slow, agonizing decline of their father's spirit and health that began with the news of Joseph's death. Though they tried repeatedly to comfort their father, he refused. They noticed that their father became more cautious about the activities and whereabouts of their younger brother Benjamin. They watched as his grief intensified when they returned from their first journey to Egypt without their brother Simeon. The last thing they remembered as they began their second journey to Egypt was the look on their father's face as they took Benjamin, his youngest son, away. How could they now consider the idea of returning to Canaan without their younger brother Benjamin? They had, indeed, changed!

DISCUSSION QUESTIONS

1. What are the four stages of guilt?

2. When Jacob's sons left the morning after the dinner, they did so with a huge sigh of relief. They had accomplished their purpose and were now safely on their way home. What happened to interrupt their journey and destroy their renewed sense of liberation? Why was the pledge they made unwise? What did the steward find when he searched their sacks?

3. We are told that Joseph had his silver cup planted in Benjamin's sack. Was that an act of retribution on his part? How would you characterize Joseph's intent in planting the cup?

4. Verse sixteen records Judah's confession. Remember, they did not take the silver cup. What was the focus of the sin he was confessing?

5. After the confession, Joseph informed them of the sentence for their deed (v. 17). What was the sentence, and how did it affect the emotions of his brothers?

6. With that sentence, Joseph raised the pressure to an unsustainable level. His brothers could no longer stand under the burden of guilt that they were bearing. What weighty factors did Judah address in his final plea for mercy from the governor?

CHAPTER 10

THE REVELATION

GENESIS 45

UP UNTIL THIS POINT, JOSEPH had been listening carefully to Judah's plea while still controlling his emotions. He was analyzing what he was hearing to see if his brothers' attitudes had actually changed. Judah's words yielded two very important revelations:

Judah and his brothers had acknowledged the impact of God's work of conviction in their hearts. No longer were they seeking to hide their sin. Judah's statement that "God hath found out the iniquity of thy servants" (Gen. 44:16) was an obviously heartfelt confession. They had also made it very clear that they were far more concerned about what would happen to their brother Benjamin and their father than what might happen to them. Hatred and bitterness were gone, and in their place were love and commitment.

Human willpower has its limitations. Joseph had been able to accomplish what Judah could not do: he was able to deal with the circumstances concerning his brothers with composure, controlling his emotions and listening to their explanations while appearing to be no more than a disinterested government administrator who cared only for protecting all that belonged to Pharaoh. Yet it was obvious that something had changed in Joseph's heart after he heard Judah's confession.

Judah and his brothers had been waiting before the governor for some time when Joseph finally responded. Joseph's first statement was startling: "Cause every man to go out from me" (Gen. 45:1). Every Egyptian in the room was dismissed, and Joseph was left standing alone with his brothers. The last time they met this way, Joseph's brothers had devised a plan to get rid of him. Earlier, in their first meeting with Joseph (without Benjamin), they had acknowledged to themselves that they had observed "the anguish of his soul, when he besought [them], and [they] would not hear" (Gen. 42:21) Now they waited and watched in astonishment as the governor of Egypt exploded with emotion, crying so loudly that those whom he had dismissed could hear him clearly.

Joseph's first statement was startling, but his second statement was terrifying: "I am Joseph. Doth my father yet live?" (Gen. 45:3). Once again, the guilt came flooding in with a vengeance, this time mixed with palpable fear. If true, several troublesome questions now had answers. But a new, more agonizing question arose: how will he avenge their treatment of him?

This is the sixth meeting Judah and his brothers have attended with the governor of Egypt. This meeting, however, was very different from the others. For the first time, Judah and his brothers are meeting with the governor alone. There were no Egyptians in the room. There was obviously something personal about their dealings with the governor of which they were not aware. For the first time, they watched as the governor yielded to his emotions, weeping uncontrollably in their presence. Why would the governor weep? Perhaps he had been deeply moved by Judah's plea. For the first time, they heard the governor speak to them in their native tongue. All previous communication had been conducted through an interpreter. They now knew that the governor understood their tongue. Every word they uttered in his presence, he heard and understood. And, for the first time, they learned the true identity of the governor.

By this time, Joseph's brothers were speechless; and it wasn't just their fear. They simply did not know how to respond to the information they had just received. What they did know was that the man in whose presence they stood had unlimited power in Egypt. They knew that he had accused them falsely and treated them roughly. They also had reason to believe that if he was, indeed, their brother Joseph, they were likely facing severe retribution.

Then Joseph spoke again: "Come near to me, I pray you" (v. 4). For Joseph to invite them to come close to him must have seemed strange. The normal practice was that Egyptians kept their distance from the Hebrews, yet the governor of Egypt was inviting them to come close. When Joseph met his brothers when they came to buy food for the first time, we are told that Joseph made himself "strange" to them. Now, he was seeking to make himself familiar to them. The idea was for them to get close enough that they could see his face clearly. Once they got close to him, he said again, "I am Joseph, your brother, whom ye sold into Egypt" (v. 4).

If a question remained about the validity of his claim to be their brother, it was answered at that moment. Only Joseph could have known the details of that night so long ago when they bartered their brother to rid themselves of this "dreamer."

Earlier, when Judah and his brothers returned from Canaan with their younger brother Benjamin, Joseph had asked: "Is your father well, the old man of whom ye spake? Is he yet alive?" (Gen. 43:27). Then Joseph repeated the question when he revealed his identity, asking, "Doth my father yet live?" (Gen. 45:3). Their father and Joseph's father were the same man. Finally, everything began to make sense. This was their brother Joseph.

Joseph wanted his brothers to understand that God had an eternal purpose in what took place. Yes, they did sell him into Egypt; but God used that event to preserve lives, theirs included. In the next four verses, we have an account of Joseph's explanation to them regarding what God had done, concluding with the statement: "So now it was not you that sent me hither, but God" (v. 8).

There are some who refer to this event as a "reunion." Yet reunions are usually planned events that are eagerly anticipated by all who are involved.

Judah and his brothers were unwilling participants in this reunion. Nor was the reunion complete. Joseph had not seen his father or the rest of his family for over twenty years.

Others call this event a "reconciliation." Joseph made it clear that he did not hold his brothers' sin against them. His forgiveness was real. Yet reconciliation requires that all barriers between the parties involved be removed. Joseph's brothers still had some issues to clear up with their father regarding what happened to Joseph more than twenty years earlier. While tears flowed and expressions of love were exchanged, more than seventeen years would pass before their reconciliation would be complete.

THE JOURNEY HOME

It was time for Joseph's brothers to return to Canaan, and this trip would be very different. They were all, Simeon and Benjamin included, making the journey; and they had good news to share with their father: "Joseph is alive, and he wants you to come and dwell near him in the land of Goshen, a country in Egypt. While the famine we are experiencing will continue for the next five years, we will not have to worry about food or provisions because Joseph will provide those things for us." It all sounded great; but there were some realities they must face, along with questions that would have to be answered.

Scripture does not record the encounters, but it does give us a bit of insight into the exchanges that must have occurred between Jacob and his sons when they returned. And while the news was good, the accountability would be difficult. Jacob would have questions, some of which would be very hard to answer: how can Joseph be alive? You brought me his coat twenty years ago and led me to believe he had been killed by a wild animal. And how do you know that Joseph is alive now, and why should I believe you? Even more astounding was the idea that Joseph somehow had the ability to provide land and provisions for us to live in Egypt. How does Joseph know the famine will last for five more years?

The answer to the first question was a problem. It required them to acknowledge their sin a second time; and this time, it was twofold. The first sin had to do with what they did to their brother Joseph and why they did it. Motives and intent had to be acknowledged along with the deed that satisfied the evil desire. They had to confess their hatred for Joseph because of his favored status with their father as well as the offense associated with his dreams. The intent was to find a way to get rid of him. The deed was accomplished by selling him to a group of peddlers passing by on their way to Egypt.

The second sin was more difficult to acknowledge because it revealed a lack of concern for their father. They deceived him for selfish reasons, discounting his love for Joseph and ignoring the overwhelming sorrow that would consume their father for years to come because of Joseph's death.

Joseph had given them answers to the other questions ahead of time. The answer to question two is found in verse twelve: "Behold, your eyes see, and the eyes of my brother Benjamin, that it is my mouth that speaketh to you." The brothers had seen Joseph and talked to him, and Benjamin can confirm that he was really his brother. The other two questions can be answered with one statement: "Thus sayeth thy son Joseph, God hath made me lord of all Egypt" (Gen. 45:9).

Though their conversation is not recorded in Scripture, Jacob's reaction is. The Scripture tells us that "Jacob's heart fainted, for he believed them not" (Gen. 45:26). The implication is that he either came very close to or did have a mild heart attack. Jacob obviously needed some evidence to support what his sons were telling him. Fortunately, his sons had evidence.

Pharaoh had learned that Joseph's brothers had come and was thrilled with the news, so much so that he issued a command to Joseph that confirmed what Joseph had already told them. They would receive land for their homes in Goshen and "eat the fat of the land" (Gen. 45:18). He also commanded that they take wagons out of Egypt for their children and wives and that they were to return to Egypt with their father. Then he added one extraordinary bit of information: "Also regard not your stuff; for the good of all the land of Egypt is yours" (Gen. 45:20).

When Jacob's sons arrived, they came with royal chariots filled with provisions to transport them back to Egypt. To each man, Joseph had given a new change of clothing (recalling that Joseph's brothers had taken his coat from him when they sold him more than twenty years earlier), but Benjamin again received special attention. Jacob's youngest son received three hundred pieces of silver and five changes of clothing.

Joseph's father also learned of the generosity of the governor of Egypt. There were ten donkeys loaded with the wealth of Egypt, along with ten other donkeys bearing corn, bread, and meat for the journey.

When Jacob heard the words and saw the treasures, his heart revived and he said, "It is enough; Joseph, my son is yet alive: I will go and see him before I die" (Gen. 45:28).

DISCUSSION QUESTIONS

1. Chapter forty-five begins with Joseph's response to Judah's plea. It is apparent that Joseph's testing has been effective. What two things was Joseph able to discern from Judah's emotional plea?

2. How did Joseph respond? Why was he so emotional?

3. After dismissing all Egyptians from the room, Joseph revealed his identity to his brethren. How did Joseph's brothers react to this revelation? Why were they troubled?

4. Why did Joseph ask them to come near him?

5. Returning home with Simeon and Benjamin was a cause for great joy, but there would be some anxiety as well. Why would they be uneasy about greeting their father with the good news?

6. What was Jacob's immediate response when his sons told him that Joseph was alive? What finally convinced him that what they told him was true?

CHAPTER 11
THE REUNION

GENESIS 46

FOR MORE THAN TWENTY YEARS, Jacob had been living with constant sorrow. Joseph was dead! Every day brought a remembrance of that reality, and every day left Jacob without a reason to live. Then came the famine and the assumed loss of his son Simeon. Sending Benjamin on the second journey to Egypt to buy grain didn't help things. Jacob was certain he would never see him again, and he blamed God for all of it.

One of the hallmarks of Jacob's grandfather Abraham was that he walked by faith. Yet Jacob had lived without faith for years, manipulating events to gain an advantage and deceiving people to benefit himself, all while leaving God out of the equation. He had become a miserable old man sitting in his chair waiting to die.

It is significant, therefore, that the first place he stopped as he began his journey to Egypt was Beersheba. He was living in Beersheba when he stole his brother Esau's blessing and birthright. But his purpose in stopping is also noteworthy. He is there to offer sacrifices unto the God of his father Isaac. It was not only his heart that had been revived; his faith had been rediscovered as well.

It didn't take long for God to make His presence known once again. God spoke to Jacob on the first night in a vision and gave him four clear promises:

1. "And he said, I am God, the God of thy father: fear not to go down into Egypt; for I will there make of thee a great nation" (Gen. 46:3). God is restating the promise that He had made years earlier to his grandfather Abraham and repeated to his father Isaac. It is a reference to the beginning of a nation for which he (Jacob) bears the name Israel.

2. "I will go down with thee into Egypt" (Gen. 46:4a). There is no way to know just how long it had been since Jacob had had any sense of God's presence in his life. For years, he had shut God out. How joyful it must have been to Jacob to have the assurance of God's presence with him in Egypt.

3. "I will also surely bring thee up again" (Gen. 46:4b). The message is that Israel (the nation, Jacob's seed) would one day leave Egypt and return to the land of promise.

4. "Joseph shall put his hand upon thine eyes" (Gen. 46:4c). This promise had a special meaning for Jacob. For the last seventeen years of his life, Jacob would enjoy a close relationship with the son that he once thought to be dead, and Joseph would be the one to close Jacob's eyes when he died.

Finally convinced of God's blessing on their plans, Jacob continued his journey with all of his family—sons, grandsons, daughters, wives, and granddaughters along with their cattle and belongings—to that special place in Egypt reserved for them by the governor, second in command only to Pharaoh. There were seventy people in all, counting Joseph's two sons Ephraim and Manasseh. A full accounting is found in Genesis 46:8-27.

Jacob must have been full of anticipation as the caravan neared its destination. It seems that any anxieties or uncertainties he may have had about what happened between Joseph and the rest of his sons had been resolved. Trust had been restored; and Jacob sent Judah ahead to meet with Joseph, who gave them specific directions to Goshen. Then Joseph went to meet his family in their new home.

It seems a bit strange that a reunion of such significance would warrant such a small accounting in Scripture. The report contains only three statements and consumes only three verses in scripture. We can be sure, however, that the time that passed got lost in the drama of the event.

The first thing we notice is that Joseph "presented himself unto [his father" (Gen. 46:29a). I'm sure the initial meeting must have taken a few moments. Joseph looked very different than he did the last time Jacob had seen him. When Joseph disappeared, he was just seventeen years old; now, he is over thirty. The last time Jacob saw him, he was wearing his "coat of many colors"; now, he is dressed in fine clothing, which identifies him as Egyptian royalty. His head and face were clean-shaven, and he arrived in a royal chariot. Jacob would have needed some time to process what he was seeing. You will remember that Joseph's brothers took some time before they were willing to approach him when they were told who he was.

Then Joseph "fell on his [father's] neck, and wept" (Gen. 46:29b). After the initial pause for recognition came the time for intimacy. Joseph once again let his emotions flow freely as he greeted his aging father, weeping on his neck for "a good while." No words were recorded because no words were needed. How do you express such joy and affection in human language? They stood there without shame for an unspecified period of time.

And finally, Jacob spoke to Joseph, and he said, "Now let me die, since I have seen thy face, because thou art yet alive" (Gen. 46:30). While that may sound like a strange thing for Jacob to say, it's simply a reflection of his thoughts for the last twenty-plus years. It is the statement of a man who was convinced he would never see his favored son alive again. Every day of his life, Jacob woke up with a stark reminder that his beloved son, Joseph, was dead. Taken in that context, his comment to his son makes perfect sense. Much like the father of the prodigal son in the book of Luke, nothing else mattered, not even his own life. Joseph, his son, who had been dead, was alive!

The relief in Joseph's heart must have been, just as was his father's, overwhelming. He had also been suffering from questions about his father's welfare. The first time Joseph's brothers came to buy food, they made it clear that they were all "the sons of one man in the land of Canaan" (Gen. 42:13). At that point, he learned that his father was alive. When they returned the second time to buy food, his second question to them (after asking about their welfare) was, "Is your father well, the old man of whom ye spake? Is he yet alive?" (Gen. 43:27). Then when he finally revealed himself to his brethren, he included a question with the simple statement "I am Joseph;" he added; "doth my father yet live?" (Gen. 45:3). Joseph was living with the same fear his father had: that he may not get to see his father alive again.

PREPARING TO MEET THE KING

Joseph's next step was to establish a communications protocol for their move to Goshen. There were two issues. First, Hebrews and Egyptians were not normally socially compatible. We learned earlier that it was unacceptable for them to eat at the same table (Gen. 43:31). The problem he was addressing here had to do with a longstanding bias that the Egyptians had against shepherds: "for every shepherd is an abomination unto the Egyptians" (Gen. 46:34).

Joseph began by explaining the process. He would visit with Pharaoh first to let him know that his family had arrived. He would then explain to the king that they were shepherds by trade and that they had brought all of their flocks and their herds with them. That information would be taken more kindly coming from Joseph than if Pharaoh learned the blunt news directly from one of Joseph's brothers himself. We must remember that all of the interaction between Joseph and his brothers had taken place at the marketplace, where the grain was purchased, or at Joseph's residence. Pharaoh's knowledge of Joseph's family was the result of what he had heard;

he had never met any of them. Joseph was planning to present his brothers to Pharaoh; and when he did, they would be introduced as Hebrew shepherds.

Add to that the fact that when Joseph first appeared to Pharaoh, he had shaved and changed his clothing. Because he was coming into the presence of the Egyptian king, he prepared himself appropriately (Gen. 41:14). Then, when Pharaoh chose Joseph to be his governor, things changed dramatically. Pharaoh gave Joseph his signet ring, dressed him in royal clothing, and put a gold chain around his neck. He made him to ride in a royal chariot that was second only to that of Pharaoh in beauty and required every man to bow in his presence. He gave him supreme authority in the land that allowed Joseph to make decisions and issue rulings at his own discretion. He then changed his name (his new Egyptian name was Zaphnath-paaneah) and gave him an Egyptian wife. Meanwhile, Joseph learned the Egyptian language and lived as an Egyptian (Gen. 41:37-45). Only in his worship did he remain loyal to his Hebrew lineage.

At this point, it had been at least ten years since Pharaoh had seen Joseph as anything other than an Egyptian. While he knew of Joseph's Hebrew descent, he had no reminder or reason to consider it in daily life. Now, he was going to meet Joseph's family, a country clan of Hebrew shepherds. Joseph's wisdom served him well. It was indeed prudent to prepare the king for the meeting.

DISCUSSION QUESTIONS

1. When Jacob began his journey to Egypt, he made an early stop along the way. Where did he stop, and why was that place significant to Jacob? What message did he receive from the Lord?

2. The trip to Egypt was a big event. All of Jacob's family went. How many people made the journey?

3. Each of Jacob's sons was listed along with their birth mother's name. What is the significance of the listing in verse nineteen? How is it different from the other listings identifying the mothers of Jacob's sons?

4. The account in Scripture of Jacob's reunion with his son Joseph is quite brief. Why would the initial meeting have been difficult for Jacob? What did he say to Joseph? Did Jacob's attitude seem a bit strange for what should have been a very happy event?

5. What was Joseph's reaction to seeing his father alive for the first time after more than twenty years?

6. One of the first things Joseph did was to introduce his family to Pharaoh. Why was that a challenge? What did Joseph do to prepare his brothers for the meeting?

CHAPTER 12

THE INTRODUCTION

GENESIS 47

HEBREW SHEPHERDS ACCOMMODATED IN THE palace of the king of Egypt—what an interesting concept. Never before would such a meeting have been tolerated. Yet here it was. Once Joseph had an opportunity to inform the king of his family's arrival in Egypt, he took five of his brethren to present them to Pharaoh.

Can you picture these Hebrew men with their robes, facial hair, and bronzed skin walking through the gates into the pristine marble-trimmed halls of the royal palace? These rugged men whose lives had most recently been spent in the dry, dusty fields of Canaan found themselves passing by immaculately disposed royal guards as they made their way to the king's reception room. Once there, the king spoke. "What is your occupation?" Their answer was direct and honest: "Thy servants are shepherds, both we, and also our fathers" (Gen. 47:3).

Some commentators have noted that earlier, when Joseph was giving instructions to his brothers about their meeting with the king, he seemed to encourage them to refrain from using the word "shepherd" in their response. The implication was that Joseph wanted Pharaoh to understand that they dealt with cattle rather than sheep (Gen. 46:34). Yet Joseph had already told Pharaoh directly that his father and his brethren had brought their flocks and their herds with them from Canaan. The word "cattle" actually means a thing bought or sold and possessed, specifically livestock. It can refer to cattle or sheep. There is no reason to involve Joseph in an attempt to deceive Pharaoh about his family's occupation.

Joseph's brothers also acknowledged their position in Egypt by referring to themselves as "servants" of Pharaoh. Then they made a specific request, one that had already been granted to Joseph on behalf of his family: "For to sojourn in the land are we come . . . now therefore, we pray thee, let thy servants dwell in the land of Goshen" (Gen. 47:4).

Pharaoh's answer was directed to Joseph rather than his brothers. That seems normal because it would be necessary for Joseph to interpret the king's answer for his brothers. But Pharaoh was not answering the question Joseph's brothers had asked. He was showing grace to Joseph. It was only because they were part of Joseph's family that they would receive this wonderful benefit. What they could not attain on their own as shepherds, they were receiving because Joseph was their brother; and their brother was a friend of the king. Genesis 47:6 describes the extensive generosity of the gift: "The land of Egypt is before thee; in the best of the land make thy father and brethren to dwell; in the land of Goshen let them dwell." Then, Pharaoh added an unexpected bonus. If there were some of Joseph's brothers who were qualified, Joseph was authorized to make them rulers over Pharaoh's cattle.

Joseph could have chosen any place in Egypt for his family to live. He chose the land of Goshen. Again, it was God's wisdom and direction working in Joseph's heart to accomplish his purpose in the lives of his people. Several reasons come to mind regarding the relationship between Jacob's family and the Egyptians, which would have made living in Goshen beneficial.

First, Goshen, while still a part of Egypt, was a bit isolated from the rest of the country. Joseph's family would be able to live and work there without having to interact on a daily basis with other Egyptians who considered them to be undesirable.

We must also remember that Egypt was a land of idolatry. They didn't worship one false god; they worshipped a multitude of false gods. Living in Goshen allowed Joseph's family to worship the true God without interference from the Egyptians.

And finally, Goshen was a rich and fertile land resting on the northern border of the Nile. It was perfect for their lifestyle. While the rest of Egypt was struggling because of the famine, the Lord had given Joseph's family a home where they could prosper and multiply. When they arrived in Egypt, their number totaled seventy. When Moses led them out of Egypt, there were six hundred thousand men, not counting women and children (Exod. 12:37). God had indeed blessed Joseph's family.

JOSEPH'S FATHER MEETS THE KING

Once the meeting with Joseph's brothers ended, Joseph brought in his father and presented him to Pharaoh. Somehow, the dynamic in the room changed. It may have been because of his age or the apparent wisdom associated with age, but Jacob's presence seemed to quiet the king. Jacob spoke first, blessing the king. Then Pharaoh inquired about Jacob's age. Jacob spoke slowly and added unrequested information in his response: "The days of the years of my pilgrimage are an hundred and thirty years: few and evil have the days of the years of my life been, and have not attained unto the days of the years of the life of my fathers in the days of their pilgrimage" (Gen. 47:9).

In typical, concise form, Jacob explained that he had experienced an unusually rough life. In his evaluation, it had been too short and filled with great sorrow. He then concluded by observing that his ancestors had lived longer and more productive lives.

There is no question that Jacob's life had produced a number of trying incidents—situations that would have caused great sorrow for any man. But this is a man who, in spite of his consistent deception, meddling, and manipulation, dreamed of a ladder reaching to Heaven with the Lord standing at the top, reminding him of the promise God had made to his grandfather Abraham and his father Isaac concerning expansive portions of land and limitless numbers of people—a promise that was now passed to him (Gen. 28:10-22). This is "Jacob," whose name means "supplanter," who wrestled all night with God and had his name changed to "Israel," which means "the prince that prevails with God" (Gen. 32:24-32). The nation that would come from his loins would bear his name. It does not appear that Jacob has any understanding of God's grace and goodness in his life.

Yet here he is, sitting in a room with a son he thought was dead, receiving an undeserved gift from the king of Egypt and telling him of his miserable life. After again offering a blessing to the king, he departs to live out his life in the presence of his beloved son Joseph in the land of Goshen while watching the famine pass by. How wonderful is the marvelous grace of God?

DEALING WITH THE FAMINE

By this time, the famine had reached its pinnacle. It was so bad that "there was no bread in all the land" (Gen. 47:13). People came and bought corn until they ran out of money. The land was bankrupt—all hope was gone, and despair began to set in. So Joseph instituted a plan, in stages, that would ensure the survival of all in Egypt. In the first stage, he offered to sell them grain in exchange for their cattle (v. 16).

When the next year arrived, the people came to Joseph to remind him that they were again without bread and had no way to produce grain. Joseph already had all their livestock. They still had their land, but it was dry and desolate and of no use whatsoever. So they again made a deal with Joseph; only now, they arranged to purchase seed with their land and their freedom. They agreed to become servants of Pharaoh in exchange for grain to make bread for their families. The only exception was for the priests. They already had an agreement with Pharaoh that allowed them to receive grain in exchange for their service as priests, and they were allowed to retain possession of their lands (v. 22).

As time passed, the famine passed; and the land began to produce again, allowing Joseph to once more establish a plan that would allow every family in Egypt to grow the food necessary to feed their family. There would be a special disbursement of seed to each of the families at no cost to them. They were to use that seed to grow a crop; and when they harvested that crop, they would give "the fifth part" to Pharaoh. Everything was collected and dispensed from the same central marketplace in Egypt. Allowing Joseph to manage the grain during the famine turned out to be a great blessing to every Egyptian. Continuing that process made it possible to distribute the grain fairly and compassionately.

Joseph's plan had worked to perfection. For seven years, he had stored up grain to prepare for the coming famine. For seven years, he had been able to supply grain for everyone in Egypt. Now, he has been able to provide a way for the Egyptians to regain their land and become prosperous once again.

The response of the people demonstrated their approval. "And they said, Thou hast saved our lives: let us find grace in the sight of my lord, and we will be Pharaoh's servants. And Joseph made it a law over the land of Egypt unto this day, that Pharaoh should have the fifth part; except the land of the priests only, which became not Pharaoh's" (Gen. 47:25-26). They had survived the famine. Joseph had led the way. And they were grateful!

JACOB'S BURIAL PLANS

At the end of the famine, Genesis 47:27 tells us, "And Israel dwelt in the land of Egypt, in the country of Goshen; and they had possessions therein, and grew, and multiplied exceedingly." For the first time in Scripture, we see Jacob's family referred to as "Israel." This is the nation that God had promised to establish through Jacob. Its size at this time is undisclosed. What we do know is that they "multiplied exceedingly." While the Egyptians were selling their cattle, land, and themselves into servitude, the infant nation of Israel was actively at work in the land of Goshen, prospering and growing.

Seventeen years had passed since Jacob's arrival in Israel. Surely, these had been some of the best years of his life. All of his sons were living there with him and apparently working together without any bitterness toward each other. Seventeen years passed without them carrying the weight of a guilty heart. No concerns about famine or want clouded their lives. It must have been a joyful time indeed.

It had been almost forty years since Jacob had borne the burden of learning that his son, his favored son Joseph, had been torn in pieces by a wild animal. When he heard the news, he vowed that he would "go down unto the grave unto my son mourning" (Gen. 37:35). But now he is calling that very same son, Joseph, in to ask for him to fulfill a very special request. He asks Joseph to make a vow that he will take his body to be buried in the cave at Machpelah in Canaan, where lie the bodies of his ancestors, Abraham and Sarah, Isaac and Rebekah, and his first wife Leah.

While it is certain that there was a sentimental reason why Jacob wanted to be buried with his ancestors, it is also likely that Jacob had a stronger motivation—a desire that was driven by a commitment to his rediscovered faith. The land of Canaan was the Promised Land, the future home of the nation that now bore his name. He longed to be buried in the land of Israel. Joseph's response was both compassionate and undeniable. His father, whom he loved so dearly, whom he had wondered about for so many years and now cared for so tenderly, would be laid to rest in Canaan.

DISCUSSION QUESTIONS

1. The first introduction Joseph made of his family to Pharaoh included five of his brothers. Why was this meeting out of character for both Joseph's brothers and Pharaoh?

2. Joseph's brothers had been coached by Joseph concerning their response to Pharaoh's questions. Pharaoh asked them about their occupation. While they answered that question, their reply was much broader in scope. What additional information did Joseph's brothers include, and why was it important for them to do so? How did Pharaoh respond to their answer? Why did he speak directly to Joseph rather than his brothers?

3. Jacob's introduction to Pharaoh followed that of his sons. How did Jacob answer Pharaoh's question to him?

4. What did Jacob's response reveal about his understanding of God's blessing in his life?

5. How was Jacob's conversation with Pharaoh different from that of his sons?

6. The famine that caused Jacob to send his sons to Egypt was far from over, and the citizens of Egypt were suffering. How did Jacob and his family fare during the final years of the famine?

7. How did Joseph's leadership provide grain and guidance to the Egyptian people for the duration of the famine?

8. What request did Jacob make of Joseph regarding his death and burial?

CHAPTER 13

THE BLESSINGS

GENESIS 48

THE JACOB THAT LAY DYING in his bed was a different man than the one who settled in Goshen seventeen years earlier. The man who came from Canaan was a man full of disappointment over the experiences of his life, a life which he then characterized as being short and miserable. The man in the bed was longing to return to Canaan, and his thoughts were focused squarely on his God.

Sometime after securing Joseph's promise to bury him in Canaan, Jacob became sick; and Joseph learned about it. So Joseph got his two sons, Ephraim and Manasseh, and took them to see their grandfather. Jacob's first words to Joseph demonstrated the change that had taken place in Jacob's heart: "God almighty appeared unto me at Luz in the land of Canaan, and blessed me, And said unto me, Behold, I will make thee fruitful, and multiply thee, and I will make of thee a multitude of people; and will give this land to thy seed after thee for an everlasting possession" (Gen. 48:3-4).

Jacob had known of that promise for years, yet it had little impact on his life. He lived as if God had forgotten him. Now, however, he has had the opportunity to see the beginning of the fulfillment of that promise. Jacob's family had grown dramatically and showed no evidence of slowing down. It was time for Joseph's sons to gain official standing in that family. Jacob makes it clear that he considers Joseph's sons to be his seed: "And now thy two sons, Ephraim and Manasseh, which were born unto thee in the land of Egypt before I came unto thee into Egypt are mine; as Reuben and Simeon, they shall be mine" (Gen. 48:5).

In verse seven, we find Jacob reminiscing tenderly about a very difficult day. He calls to mind the death of Rachel. Though she was his second wife, she was his first and only true love. In verse twenty-seven of chapter forty-four, when Judah was pleading with Joseph for the life of Benjamin, he repeats what his father, Jacob, had said to him: "You know that my wife bare me two sons." Jacob had always considered Rachel to be his only wife. He remembers that they almost made it to Bethlehem. They had to bury her along the way. Joseph was Rachel's firstborn and, as such, deserved the blessing of the firstborn; so he received a double portion, and each of his sons was given a separate allotment in the land of Canaan.

Then Israel noticed Joseph's sons in the room, though he didn't recognize them. For the first time, we learn that Israel's vision had begun to deteriorate. Jacob would have remembered the day many years earlier when he deceived his father, Isaac, whose eyes were also dim, stealing his older brother Esau's blessing. (God did use that transaction, however, to accomplish His purpose and see that Jacob received the blessing of the firstborn.) Israel, however, would be careful to avoid any hint of deceit, making sure to follow God's leading with Joseph's sons.

Once Joseph reminded him who they were, Israel called Ephraim and Manasseh to come close "and he kissed them, and embraced them" (Gen. 48:10). Then he spoke to Joseph: "I had not thought to see thy face: and, lo, God hath shown me also thine seed (v. 11).

Now, the transformation from Jacob to Israel had been accomplished. The memories of a life of few years and much evil had been replaced with a recognition of the goodness of God and a heart filled with overwhelming gratitude. From this point on, the term "Israel" would no longer refer to a man. Instead, it was the God-ordained name of the nation that proceeded from his loins.

Joseph brought his two sons to Israel, Ephraim, the youngest, before Israel's left hand, and Manasseh, the oldest, before his father's right hand. Then something unexpected happened. Israel crossed his hands as he began his blessing, placing his right hand on Ephraim's head and his left hand on Manasseh's head. The Bible says that he "guided his hands wittingly" (v. 14). This was not the first time that God had moved a father to select the younger son over the older. Israel was now filling that role because of God's intervention. Joseph objected, and Israel made it clear that he knew what he doing and would not be reconsidering his choice (v. 17-19).

Verses fifteen and sixteen, along with verse twenty, record the details of God's blessing on Joseph and his sons. The tribe of Ephraim, though younger, would be the superior tribe. Manasseh would occupy a lesser position of great honor as well. Verse twenty sums it up as Israel says, "In thee shall Israel bless, saying, God make thee as Ephraim and Manasseh: and he set Ephraim before Manasseh."

Israel concluded his visit with Joseph and his sons with a brief statement of his impending death. He speaks of it as if it is a comfortable ending to a pleasant journey rather than an unfriendly termination to a miserable life in which "all these things are against me" (Gen. 42:36). Seventeen years in the land of Goshen had changed his perspective.

He then assures them of God's abiding presence and reconfirms that one day, they would return to inhabit the land of his fathers. Those promises were significant. Israel's faith had become sight. The nation of Israel was no longer a dream. They were living temporarily in a foreign land and would endure much difficulty before finally returning to the land that Israel loved so dearly; but the journey had begun, and his son Joseph would lead the way.

DISCUSSION QUESTIONS

1. Chapter forty-eight begins with Jacob dealing with sickness. Upon learning his father was sick, Joseph took his two sons to visit him. What did Jacob's initial statement to Joseph reveal about his perspective as he reflected on the years of his "pilgrimage?"

2. How did Jacob view the status of Joseph's sons Ephraim and Manasseh in his lineage?

3. Verse eight identifies Jacob as "Israel." What does that name change reveal about Jacob's status with the Lord?

4. When Israel began to bless his grandsons, he put his right hand on Ephraim, the youngest, and his left hand on the older son Manasseh. Why did Joseph protest that action? How died Israel react when Joseph protested?

5. How is this process different from the blessing that Jacob received from his father Isaac? Why is that difference significant?

6. The chapter closes with Israel acknowledging that death is near. He also reveals a twofold prophecy regarding God's plan for Joseph and the nation of Israel. What were the two tenets of that prophecy? Why were they important to Joseph's future?

CHAPTER 14

THE PROPHECIES

GENESIS 49

CHAPTER FORTY-NINE BEGINS BY TELLING us that "Jacob" called his sons together. In chapter forty-eight, as Joseph's father blessed his grandsons, his name is mentioned seven times; and each time, Joseph's father was identified as "Israel." Why does Scripture change the designation in verse one of chapter forty-nine?

Up until this time, the name "Israel" could refer to a man who used to be named Jacob or to a new nation that would soon be formed. But at this time, the new nation has already been established. Small though it was, "Israel," the nation, was prospering and growing at an astounding rate. Exodus 1:7 describes the growth of Israel after just one generation: "And the children of Israel were fruitful, and increased abundantly, and multiplied, and waxed exceeding mighty; and the land was filled with them."

Could it be that the man "Israel" ("prince who has power with God") fulfilled his last responsibility when he helped solidify the nation of Israel by blessing Joseph's sons? The man "Jacob" ("supplanter") could not have done that. And who would be the one to carry out the responsibility of prophecy for Jacob's sons? The prophecy recalls events in the lives of Jacob's sons that were anything but worthy of "Israel's" attention. "Jacob" would need to carry out that chore. Then he would die, and "Israel" would be permanently established as the covenant name of the people of God.

PROPHECIES OR BLESSINGS?

There are two opinions about the content recorded in Genesis 49. Some believe it all refers to blessings. Others think these declarations regarding Jacob's sons are primarily prophecies. The second opinion is supported by Jacob's statement when he called his sons together in verse one: "Gather yourselves together, that I may tell you that which shall befall you in the last days."

Prophecies have to do with predictions, foretelling coming events with a certain measure of specificity. Blessings carry an implication of imparting a positive gift of some kind, many times pertaining to prosperity. With the exception of his statements about Joseph, Jacob simply explained that the destiny of his sons would be determined by their history, more specifically their character, rather than by spiritual gifts bequeathed to them. In these cases, the prophecies could be considered as a natural result of the law of "sowing and reaping."

One by one, Jacob listed his sons, revealed their character, and projected their destiny.

REUBEN

Reuben was the firstborn son of Leah, Jacob's first wife. As such, he was entitled to a double portion in his inheritance. He forfeited that right because of a heinous sin; and Joseph, the firstborn son of Jacob's second wife Rachel, received it instead. Reuben's character was revealed in all its gruesome disgust and his prophecy was very brief and to the point: "thou shalt not excel" (v. 4).

SIMEON AND LEVI

Simeon and Levi were joined together in their prophecy because they were brothers and because of the similarities of their character and their companionship in crime. They were the instigators of a brutal and unjust slaughter of innocent people in an attempt to exact revenge for a crime against their sister. Jacob characterized what they did as "fierce" and "cruel." Simeon was to receive no inheritance in the land, instead being "divided" in Jacob. Over time, they became absorbed by a number of other tribes. Levi became the priestly tribe. As such, they were "scattered" in Israel. They had forty-eight cities where they lived and ministered among the tribes. The natural result was that they would never have an opportunity to conspire together in any activity again (v. 5-7).

JUDAH

Judah was also a son of Leah. He was the primary advocate for Joseph's survival when his brothers determined to rid themselves of the "dreamer," though it would have meant more if he had not accomplished it by encouraging them to sell him into bondage. Then there was the ugly incident with Tamar, and he had married a pagan woman. Why Jacob chose to overlook these things in the life of Judah is left to our speculation. Perhaps Judah found pardon because he stepped forward to plead for the life of Benjamin when Joseph's silver cup was found in his sack. At any rate, Judah was given a pass on his sins. Judah's selection as the tribe of royalty meant that he would be the root of the Messianic line. Verse ten states, "The sceptre shall not depart from Judah, Nor a lawgiver from between his feet, Until Shiloh come; And unto him shall the gathering of the people be." The throne of Israel would be occupied by kings from many tribes; but at the end, the "Lion of the tribe of Judah" (Shiloh) will appear and take His rightful place upon that throne for eternity. Verses eleven and twelve point to a time of universal peace and prosperity when Israel finally receives all of the land they have been promised when the Messiah establishes His millennial kingdom.

ZEBULUN

We know little of Zebulun except that he was Leah's youngest son. Zebulun's destiny included property upon the seacoast stretching to Zidon, a wealthy city along the Mediterranean coasts. When that prophecy was or will be fulfilled is unknown. It's possible that this prophecy could be fulfilled in the millennium (v. 13).

ISSACHAR

Issachar is characterized as being strong and adept at bearing burdens. Verses fourteen and fifteen describe a stable, dependable people who carried their burdens with distinction. They were not known for heroics, nor is there any evidence of evil or wickedness.

DAN

Dan was the first son of Bilhah, Rachel's handmaid. Judges arose from the tribe of Dan to judge the nation of Israel, most notably Samson. The people of Dan were shrewd and cunning, but they also made graven images and engaged in brazen idolatry (Judg. 18:30-31).

GAD

Zilpah, Leah's handmaid, was the mother of Gad. Gad is one of two tribes who claimed a possession outside of the Promised Land (Reuben was the other). The location gave the enemy ample opportunity to attack. Thus, the prophecy in verse nineteen states that "a troop shall overcome him: but he shall overcome at last."

ASHER

Asher was Gad's brother, also born to Zilpah. The tribe of Asher occupied one of the most fertile lands in Canaan. The statement in verse twenty—"his bread shall be fat and he shall yield royal dainties"—foretold a bounty of rich food that would grace the tables of kings.

NAPHTALI

Naphtali is Dan's brother, also born to Rachel's handmade Bilhah. The prophecy pictures a "hind let loose" that "giveth goodly words" (v. 21). The picture is of a deer running freely and fluency of speech (some have suggested poetry). Naphtali was one of two tribes (the other was Zebulun) commended for courage and sacrifice in battle (Judg. 5:18).

JOSEPH

Finally, Jacob gets to the sons of Rachel. There was never any question that she was Jacob's favorite wife, and he never made an effort to hide it. He had spent fourteen years of his life earning the right to marry her, and his love for her never waned. Her sons would also receive the benefit of that favor. Jacob's comments about Joseph do reflect his character, but the prophecies that follow abound with special blessings that will impact Joseph's future. Looking at Joseph must have caused a sense of gratitude and tenderness to well up in Jacob's heart. He was obviously remembering the years of sorrow that he endured after losing him. And now here he stands, governor of Egypt and faithful provider for the entire family/nation. Without him, they would have perished. Without him, they would not be standing here today. So much to say, but so hard to say it.

Jacob first compares Joseph to a fruitful branch on a tree that drew water from a nearby well. So prosperous was this branch that it spilled over the wall beside it. Because Joseph received a double portion in Israel (one each to Ephraim and Manasseh), his fruitfulness would be doubled.

Yet Joseph's journey in life was not always pleasant. The archer's attack hearkens back to the day of the pit when his brothers hated him enough to barter him away as a slave. Nor would Ephraim and Manasseh escape the arrows of the archers. They would have to fight valiantly to secure their inheritance in Canaan: "But his bow abode in strength, And the arms of his hands were made strong By the hands of the mighty God of Jacob; (From thence is the shepherd, the stone of Israel:)" (v. 24). Though the archers attacked Joseph aggressively, his bow remained strong because of his faithful trust in his God. God gave him the strength to endure the hatred and unjust treatment of his brothers and face the temptation of Potiphar's wife without compromising his integrity or sinning against his God. He dealt with two unjust years of prison without complaining, knowing that the God Who had protected him thus far would keep him safe until his purpose was fulfilled. God was his Shepherd and his Rock. His conviction never faltered, and his heart never doubted. Surely, the "mighty God of Jacob" had, indeed, made him strong.

Jacob then assured Joseph that his sons would be the recipient of an abundance of blessings from Heaven above and from the depths below, blessings of the breasts and of the womb. Ephraim and Manasseh would be fertile tribes, whose numbers would increase dramatically in the years to come. Then Jacob said something amazing. He corrected the ugly, misguided statement he had made earlier to Pharaoh when he said, "Few and evil have the days of the years of my life been, and have not attained unto the days of the years of the life of my fathers in the days of their pilgrimage" (Gen. 47:9). The only ones who heard that statement besides the Lord were Pharaoh and Joseph.

He then said to Joseph, "The blessings of thy father have prevailed above the blessings of my progenitors unto the utmost bound of the everlasting hills:" (Gen. 49:26a). He may not have lived longer than his grandfather Abraham (175 years) or his father Isaac (180 years), but he has been blessed far beyond either of them. The fulfillment of God's promise to all of them was now in progress, and Jacob had lived to see his dream born. Those same blessings of abundance would extend to Joseph, the son "that was separate from his brethren" (v. 26b). Joy and gratitude filled the heart of Jacob, a consequence of God's goodness in his life, much of which he had not seen before and didn't understand because of the emptiness of his faith. Now he can see. His eyes have been opened. Jacob is blessing Joseph as well as engaging in an act of worship as he remembers the bounty of the last seventeen years.

BENJAMIN

Benjamin was Jacob's youngest son. His mother, Rachel, died while giving him life. The references to a "wolf," "prey," and "spoil" (v. 27) all depict Benjamin as a strong, warring tribe. Ehud, the judge, was of the tribe of

Benjamin (Judg. 3:15), as was Saul, the first king of Israel and Saul of Tarsus in the New Testament, who, while traveling on the road to Damascus, became the apostle Paul.

While verse twenty-eight indicates that Jacob blessed all of his sons, he must have done so in a very general way because the only specific blessings mentioned were those pertaining to Joseph. He was so full of gratitude as he recalled God's blessing that it would have been a simple thing to offer a blanket blessing to them all at the end.

JACOB'S DEATH

As Jacob's journey in life came to an end, his heart turned toward home; and he looked back to that field in the land of Canaan, where his family was buried. It was a simple cave that his grandfather Abraham had purchased from Ephron the Hittite. His grandfather was there, along with his grandmother Sarah, his father Isaac, his mother Rebekah, and his first wife Leah. His sons must take him there to be buried. Then, with a simplicity that belies the life he lived, Jacob "gathered up his feet into the bed, and yielded up the ghost, and was gathered to his people" (v. 33).

DISCUSSION QUESTIONS

1. In verse one of chapter forty-nine, the Scripture once again uses Jacob's birth name to identify him as he begins to tell his sons what shall befall them in the last days. Why do you think the Scripture reverts to calling him "Jacob"?

2. What is the difference between a "prophecy" and a blessing?"

3. How were Jacob's comments concerning Joseph and Benjamin different from those concerning his other sons?

4. What was Jacob's primary concern as he was dying?

CHAPTER 15

THE RECONCILIATION

GENESIS 50

IT HAD BEEN ALMOST FORTY years since Joseph had dealt with the death of a family member. He was there along the road to Ephrath when his mother died giving birth to Benjamin. But this was different. Joseph had now lost his father twice: first when his brothers sold him into slavery and now, a second time. Seeing his father lying on his deathbed was too much for Joseph. He was overwhelmed with grief. Scripture tells us that Joseph "fell upon his father's face and wept upon him, and kissed him" (Gen. 50:1). They then embalmed him: "And forty days were fulfilled for him; for so are fulfilled the days of those which are embalmed: and the Egyptians mourned for him threescore and ten days" (v. 3). Then Joseph began preparations to go to Canaan to bury his father.

Jacob was evidently a well-respected resident of Egypt. It would be natural for all of Jacob's family to mourn his death, but for the Egyptians to mourn him for seventy days would be unnatural. Jacob was a Hebrew and a shepherd, both of which were considered undesirable in Egypt. But he was also Joseph's father, and Joseph's stature in Egypt made Joseph's father more than worthy of the honor.

Though Joseph was governor of Egypt and had authority over all the land, he still had a job to do for which he was accountable to the king. Leaving that responsibility for an extended time required more authority than he had; so he sent messengers to Pharaoh to seek permission to go and bury his father in the land of Canaan, fulfilling the vow he had made to his father and promising that he would return. Pharaoh did not need to see Joseph, so he sent word for Joseph to go and bury his father.

JACOB'S BURIAL

The processional that left Egypt for Canaan included more than Jacob's family. Joining in the convoy were "all the servants of Pharaoh, the elders of his house and all the elders of the land of Egypt" (v. 7). They were accompanied by chariots and horsemen. Though we don't have an exact number, verse nine describes it as "a very great company." The only ones who did not make the trip were the children and animals that were a part of Jacob's family.

As they crossed the Jordan River, they stopped at the threshing floor of Atad. For seven days, they mourned and lamented Jacob's death. It must have been quite a spectacle, this group of Hebrews and Egyptians joining together to grieve over the death of a 147-year-old Hebrew shepherd. The Canaanites in the vicinity took note of the ceremony and concluded that this must have been a highly respected Egyptian dignitary. Perhaps we should take time here to remember who is in the coffin and why the Egyptians have given him such honor and why the Canaanites were so amazed. He was the fulfillment of an ancient promise given to his grandfather Abraham and his father Isaac. He was the father of a nation that bears his name today. His name was "Israel."

The last leg of the journey took Joseph and his brothers to their final destination, the cave in the field of Machpelah, where they buried their father. After rejoining the group, they returned to Egypt.

COMPLETE RECONCILIATION

The trip back must have been a bit uncomfortable for Joseph's brothers. Echoes of previous trips from Canaan to Egypt and back began to cloud their mind. Guilt, fear, and speculation abounded as they wondered what Joseph might do now that their father was dead, and the old, nagging uncertainty about Joseph's desire to get even returned. They were sure their father was their only source of protection, and now he was gone. It made sense to keep their distance from Joseph. Their plan, likely concocted on their way home, had a familiar theme. When they sold their brother into slavery, they deceived their father about Joseph. This time, they turned it around—they deceived Joseph about something their father (had not) said.

> And when Joseph's brethren saw that their father was dead, they said, Joseph will peradventure hate us, and will certainly requite us all the evil which we did unto him. And they sent a messenger unto Joseph, saying, Thy father did command before he died, saying, So shall ye say unto Joseph, Forgive, I pray thee now, the trespass of thy brethren, and their sin; for they did unto thee evil: and now, we pray thee, forgive the trespass of the servants of the God of thy father. And Joseph wept when they spake unto him (Gen. 50:15-17).

Yet their effort to extend their father's protection beyond the grave was unnecessary. Joseph had forgiven them many years ago. He had no desire for revenge. When Joseph got their message, he sent for them and again, with tears flowing, assured them that they had been forgiven. How could they have so badly misjudged his kindness and love? For the last seventeen years, he had been their faithful shepherd, protecting, preserving, and providing for them. One last time, the Scripture records that they "fell down before his face" (v. 18).

Joseph's response communicated humility, grace, and gratitude in an attempt to dispel their fear again. His question to them—"am I in the place of God?" (v. 19)—revealed his understanding that God was in control from the beginning of the conflict. Then he said, "But as for you, ye thought evil against me; but God meant it unto good, to bring to pass, as it is this day, to save much people alive" (v. 20). Once more, he assured them of his care; "I will nourish you, and your little ones" (v. 21a). We are then told that "he comforted them, and spake kindly unto them" (v. 21b).

Joseph lived to be 110 years old and, like his father before him, requested that his bones not be left in Egypt. The children of Israel promised that they would carry his bones with them to Canaan. And the story finished with the words, "So Joseph died, being an hundred and ten years old: and they embalmed him, and he was put in a coffin in Egypt" (v. 26).

But what a story! For Joseph, there had been thirteen years of unfair treatment; and he responded with steadfast faith. Then, he had seventeen years of prosperity and power, and he responded with steadfast faith. For thirty years, he looked to God for wisdom and guidance and allowed God to use him in good times and bad.

In contrast, for thirteen years, Joseph's brothers lived without unfair treatment but had to endure the constant sorrow of a father who thought his favorite son was dead while knowing that they were responsible. They spent seventeen years in the presence of their younger brother, who provided housing and provisions for them in a fertile land in Egypt, knowing all the time that they did not deserve his kindness and wondering when they would be forced to pay for their sin. For thirty years, they looked to Joseph with hearts filled with fear and guilt.

But that's not the end of the story. For sixty-three more years, Joseph and his brothers lived together with peace and joy because of Joseph's grace and his brothers' willingness to believe that "God meant it for good" (Gen. 50:20).

DISCUSSION QUESTIONS

1. When Jacob died, we are told that "the Egyptians mourned for him for threescore and ten days (v. 4)." Why would the Egyptians mourn for a Hebrew shepherd?

2. The funeral caravan from Egypt to Canaan for Jacob's burial was quite large, including Hebrews and Egyptians. When they stopped for seven days to pay their respects to Joseph at Atad's threshing floor on the west side of Jordan, the Canaanites took notice. What conclusions did they draw concerning the man who was in the coffin?

3. With their father now buried, Joseph's brothers began to wonder what was in Joseph's mind. What concerns did they have, and how did they address them?

4. How did Joseph respond when he heard of his brother's concerns?

5. What legacy did Joseph leave for his family?

CHAPTER 16

JOSEPH'S GODLY PERSPECTIVE

THE WORD "PERSPECTIVE" HAS TO do with sight. Webster defines the word perspective as "a mental view or prospect" or "the capacity to view things in their true relations or relative importance."[2] Everyone has a perspective; and that perspective affects how they think, what they do, and how they feel. That rather influential perspective, for most people, is determined by their circumstances in life. Good circumstances lead to a positive perspective on life. Unpleasant circumstances lead to a negative perspective on their life.

JOSEPH'S CIRCUMSTANCES

Beginning our examination of Joseph's life in Genesis 37 provides a great window into the frequency and severity of his circumstances. For thirteen years, Joseph dealt with the consequences of circumstances over which he had no control. These unnatural circumstances did not occur because of his misdeeds (therefore, the principle and sowing and reaping did not apply). Nor were they the result of random, accidental events that created hardship for him. Instead, they were premeditated efforts designed to inflict harm to better the life circumstances of the perpetrators. Others were treating him badly for their anticipated benefit.

---

2   Merriam-Webster, s.v. "perspective (n.)," accessed August 5, 2024, https://www.merriam-webster.com/dictionary/perspective.

We will examine how Joseph handled all of this later; but for the moment, let's examine exactly what happened to Joseph. There were two locations with offenders in each place, one an organized group of offenders and the other a pair of individuals.

Joseph's first group of incidents came from familiar people, his brothers. The acts were fueled by favoritism from their father, Jacob, validated by a special "coat of many colors" that Joseph received. The favoritism caused intense resentment among his brothers. Remember, too, that nine of his brothers were born to three "wives" of his father who were considered inferior to Joseph's mother, which only added to their bitterness toward Joseph. Then there was the matter of Joseph's dreams. There were six incidents in all.

1. Unwarranted, passionate hatred (v. 4): Were Joseph's brothers justified in their hatred? Perhaps. Their hatred was driven by their perspective, which led them to believe that they were being mistreated. Even so, the focus of their hatred was misplaced. Joseph had done nothing (based on the account we have from Scripture) to merit such hatred. The responsibility belonged to their father.

2. Conceiving a plan to kill him (v. 20): Hatred has to reach a certain level of intensity to warrant taking another person's life. Somehow, Joseph's brothers had reached that point. Their imagination led them to believe that the fulfillment of Joseph's dreams would affect their future circumstances in a negative way. Remember that Joseph offered no interpretation of his dreams; he only shared with them the content. The anticipated outcome of those dreams terrified them and twisted their perspective.

3. Stealing his "coat of many colors" (v. 23): I've often wondered why they would want to steal his coat. It's obvious that none of them could have worn it in a public place. If they were going to kill him, what difference would it make other than to cause him

additional pain? Evidently, the pain was the desired consequence. While they did use the coat to deceive their father about Joseph's disappearance, that was not a concern in this discussion. Seeing the coat on a daily basis reminded them of their inferior status with their father. They felt their circumstances would improve if they destroyed the coat.

4. Casting him into an empty pit (v. 24): The original plan was to "slay him" and then cast him into some pit" (v. 20). But Reuben convinced them to cast him into a pit without killing him. Then Reuben could rescue him later. When he returned, he found the pit empty; and he was alarmed. He was struggling with what they were going to tell their father.

5. Depriving him of food or water (vs. 24-25): Even a prisoner who is about to die is entitled to a last meal, but Joseph's brothers were not feeling so generous. They dumped him into the pit and sat down to eat without giving Joseph another thought.

6. Selling him into bondage (vs. 25-27): Since Judah had talked them out of killing Joseph, they decided the next best thing was to sell him to a group of traveling peddlers whose destination they knew was Egypt. It would take care of two problems: ridding them of his presence and allegedly destroying any hope for the fulfillment of his dreams.

Relationship problems in families are not unusual, but those that reach to the level of murder are rare. The more astounding consequence of this situation is that Joseph never seemed to resent his brothers for what they did to him. Though his circumstances were awful, they never seemed to affect his perspective.

The problems with his brothers, however, were just the beginning. When he got to Egypt, he was again sold, this time to a man named Potiphar, who was the captain of the king's guard. While Joseph was unfairly sold into slavery, his initial encounter with slavery was not so bad. It turned out that Potiphar appreciated Joseph's character and gave him a position of great prominence. He made him overseer of all his house. Then the mistreatment started again. This time, the perpetrator was Potiphar's wife. Joseph found himself in a hopeless situation. How could he continue to please his master if he could not avoid offending his master's wife? The attack was clearly focused on one simple request: "Lie with me." This time, the attack occurred in five stages.

1. She tempted him. The Bible says that Joseph was a "goodly person, and well favored" (Gen. 39:6). I'm sure that Joseph was well favored by his master and the other servants with whom he worked. But his primary attraction was because His God had chosen to favor him. To a wicked woman, a young man who was as innocent as Joseph appeared would have been irresistible.

2. She grabbed him. After Joseph explained the reasons, both ethical and spiritual, why he could not accept her proposal, Potiphar's wife intensified the pursuit. She arranged to be alone in the house, with Joseph intending to force his hand. Whatever the outcome, it would be his word against hers. Joseph would have no recourse but to yield. When Joseph came in, she grabbed him by his coat.

3. She ordered him. The words were the same, but the intent was different. Potiphar's wife was not going to accept another rejection. When she grabbed his coat, the attack became physical; and her request had turned into a demand: "Lie with me!" Joseph had but one option available, and that was to flee. So he left his garment in her hand and escaped from the house.

4. She accused him. A privileged woman deprived of her fleshly desires seldom retains the qualities of integrity, fairness, or mercy

in her character. Potiphar's wife cared about only one thing: convincing the other servants that Joseph was the aggressor and that she barely escaped without having her virtue soiled. She told the story her way, though we can be fairly certain the servants knew the truth of the matter.

5. She imprisoned him. It may have been Potiphar who passed and carried out the sentence against Joseph, but it was his wife who was responsible. We are told in Scripture that Potiphar was angry when he heard what had happened, but we are not told who was the focus of his anger. He knew his wife's character and would have been bitterly disappointed to lose a highly skilled servant such as Joseph to satisfy his wife's hypocritical anger and pride.

Joseph spent two long years in prison for something he did not do. But once again, there seemed to be no change in Joseph's perspective. His circumstances changed, but his outlook didn't. Later, in a chapter dealing with reconciliation, we will learn that Joseph's brothers, though they tried every way possible to alter their circumstances and were somewhat successful, failed to change their perspective. Joseph took every challenge in stride, moving forward and keeping a proper focus.

JOSEPH'S PERSPECTIVE

Some people just seem to be happy even though their circumstances are bad. I once heard a missionary speak about the terrible conditions that the people on their field experienced. Their housing was almost nonexistent; they hauled water from the river; their diet consisted of what they were able to produce from their labors in the field, a small plot of land that was less than reliable because of the uncertain weather patterns where they lived. The men toiled all day in the field or at the river, and the women worked from sunup to sundown to provide meals, make or repair clothing, and look after the children. Entertainment, such as it was, consisted of time spent around the campfire in the evening before going to bed. It was the kind of existence that most of us would consider uncivilized. Yet when the missionary described living conditions in America, telling them of all the wonderful luxuries we enjoy, they responded as we would to them. They were happy where they were. Their perspective had not been falsely enhanced by unrealistic expectations.

Joseph seemed to be a happy person. Some might argue that was true because of Jacob's partiality toward him. Yet Joseph lived a great part of his life without the benefit of that partiality and still appeared to be happy. You will remember that Joseph had two dreams that became fodder for his brother's hatred. Though he would not fully understand the meaning of those dreams for many years, he would choose to embrace them as having come from God. Those dreams provided a foundation for Joseph's belief that God had a purpose for his life and his choice to simply "settle in for the ride." That did not mean that he just let things happen as they would; it meant that he would do his best in each situation he encountered to prepare himself for whatever God had in mind. Joseph chose to live by faith. His life is a perfect example of what it means to embrace the biblical expectation that "the just shall live by faith" (Heb. 10:38).

Faith is many things to many people. For some, faith represents their source of power with God. They see faith as a type of spiritual currency that they avail themselves of when they need something from the Lord. The greater their faith, the greater the response from the Lord. It is not uncommon to hear people say that their failure to get their prayer answered was due to their lack of faith. After all, did not Jesus criticize the disciples on more than one occasion for having little or no faith? He also commended the Roman centurion, whose servant he healed of the palsy for possessing "great" faith (Matt. 8:5-13). Yet on none of those occasions was Jesus dealing with the "quantity" of their faith; instead, he was talking about having faith, period.

Jesus had an interesting discussion with his apostles in Luke 17. It seems that the apostles were concerned that their faith was lacking, so they asked the Savior to "increase" their faith. Wouldn't all of us like to have more faith? And here is the Savior's response. "And the Lord said, If ye had faith as a grain of mustard seed, ye might say unto this sycamine tree, Be thou plucked up by the root, and be thou planted in the sea; and it should obey you" (Luke 17:6). Jesus seems to be saying that you don't need a great quantity of faith to see great things happen. In fact, he described the exact size of the amount of faith needed as "the size of a mustard seed."

Faith, in its simplest sense, is belief, and that belief is the foundation of our salvation. Let's take a moment to examine several familiar verses:

- "But without faith it is impossible to please him: for he that cometh to God must believe that he is, and that he is a rewarder of them that diligently seek him" (Heb. 11:6). There are two very important statements in that verse: we cannot please God without faith, and we cannot know God without faith (believing that He is).
- "Now faith is the substance of things hoped for, the evidence of things not seen" (Heb. 11:1). Notice that without faith, you will be missing certain things that are essential to our walk as believers. The substance that produces hope is found only in faith. The ability to see anticipated things that God may have promised is available only to those who have faith.
- "Through faith we understand that the worlds were framed by the word of God, so that things which are seen were not made of things which do appear" (Heb. 11:3). Understanding is lacking for those who choose not to live by faith.

Substance, hope, sight, and understanding all exist to help a believer navigate a life that is full of ups and downs, trials and tragedies, and an unending number of crooked paths leading to confusion, turmoil, and, ultimately, despair.

Do you remember our discussion regarding perspective at the beginning of this chapter? You will recall that Webster defined perspective as follows: "a mental *view* or prospect" or "the capacity to *view* things in their true relations or relative importance" (emphasis added).[3] For a believer, that perspective is a consequence of our faith, which provides substance, hope, sight, and understanding. All of these encourage confidence in our God and allow us to view the circumstances of life "in their true relations or relative importance."

Here is a spiritual definition of faith: *faith is the filter through which we view every circumstance of life, whether good or evil.* When David stood before Goliath, he viewed him through the filter of faith, and he had hope and confidence and could see clearly the victory that his God could provide. Likewise, Shadrach, Meshach, and Abed-nego had no fear of the burning fiery furnace because they knew their God could deliver them from the furnace; but they also were certain that God would deliver them from the King's hand. Scripture is filled with people who viewed their circumstances through the eyes of faith and lived as Joseph did.

But wait a minute! Faith does not provide physical sight, nor can you feel God's touch or hear His voice. That does not mean that you cannot see, touch, or hear the Lord. It just means that those personal connections with God do not take place in the physical realm. That brings us to the second part of the definition of faith. *Faith is the filter through which you learn of, get to know, and interact with God.* Without faith, we have no hope. Without faith, we cannot see. Without faith, we cannot understand. All because without faith, we have no connection with our God.

Living by faith means that believers have a healthy relationship with their God. They know Him, and He knows them. The lines of communication are always open. If we study the promises found in Scripture about our God, we can conclude that our faith can and should make certain assumptions.

---

3   Ibid.

Faith assumes God's purpose. God has a purpose and plan for every believer. Some follow God's plan, and some choose to go their own way; but the fact remains that we are here to fulfill God's purpose for our lives. We are each a special creation, and God has given us certain talents and abilities because He wants to use us in a specific way. His ultimate goal for us is clear. He is working within us to change us into the image of His dear Son. Beyond that, He wants us to draw other men to Himself. Every circumstance He allows in our lives will be for our benefit and His glory, and every event will work toward the fulfillment of His specific purpose for us.

Faith assumes God's providence. Not only is our life's purpose determined by God, but the path that leads us to our destination is also planned as well. Psalms 37:23 assures us that "the steps of a good man are ordered by the Lord." Living by faith means that we understand that God is in control, that His way is perfect, and that bumps in the road are simply part of the journey. Every challenge gets us one step closer to our earthly goal and our heavenly home.

Faith assumes God's presence. "Whither shall I go from thy spirit? Or whither shall I flee from thy presence?" That was King David's question in Psalm 139:7. If you read the entire psalm, you will see that he comes to the inevitable conclusion that avoiding the presence of God is impossible. While the question may sound like David is seeking to flee from the Lord's presence, the opposite is actually true. He is worshiping God for the assurance of His presence. In verse five, David says of his God, "Thou hast beset me behind and before, And laid thine hand upon me." Then in verse six, David erupts with a declaration of praise when he states, "Such knowledge is too wonderful for me; It is high, I cannot attain unto it." It is indeed an overwhelming realization to think that God would accompany us through every challenge that we face. Yet we are reminded in Hebrews 13:5 that "he hath said, I will never leave thee, nor forsake thee."

Faith assumes God's protection. "God is our refuge and strength, a very present help in time of trouble" (Psalm 46:1). God does not simply accompany us on our journey; He is there to help us avoid the attack of our adversary. The ever-present question is, why does God allow bad things to happen to good people? You might ask, why did God allow me to have that accident; or why didn't the Lord prevent me from contracting that disease? Joseph could have asked why the Lord allowed him to go to prison for something he didn't do. In Joseph's situation, the answer is somewhat clear. His time in prison was a Divine appointment that laid the foundation for his meeting with Pharaoh. We should also remember that if God had not protected him, he may have died. Rape in those days was a capital offense and worthy of death. To question God's protection is to surrender an indispensable benefit that our faith provides.

Faith assumes God's provision. It was David, once again, who acknowledged God's consistent provision for his saints when he said, "I have been young, and now am old; Yet I have not seen the righteous forsaken, nor his seed begging bread" (Psalm 37:25). This is one of those promises that is so prolific throughout Scripture that it is hard to believe that anyone ever missed it. Jesus advised his disciples not to worry about life, food, drink, clothing, or stature because "your heavenly father knoweth that ye have need of all these things," emphasizing that "all these things shall be added unto you" (Matt. 6:32-33). Philippians 4:6 reminds us that we are to "be careful [anxious] for nothing." Paul reminded the believers at Philippi that "my God shall supply all your need according to his riches in glory by Christ Jesus" (Phil. 4:19).

Faith assumes God's peace. There is only one way to know such peace, and that is by faith alone. Isaiah 26:3 clearly gives the lone requirement: "Thou wilt keep him in perfect peace, whose mind is stayed on thee." Joseph was able to maintain "perfect peace" because his focus was fixed on his God and what He was doing in Joseph's life.

Faith assumes God's power. One of the most difficult tasks for us as believers is to remember who is responsible for the good things that happen in our lives. We are conditioned to believe that if we do what's right, the consequence will always be positive. Yet Scripture makes it clear that we are not to expend energy doing what we think is right. Proverbs 14:12 says, "There is a way which seemeth right unto a man, But the end thereof are the ways of death." It is not our plans, our thoughts, our goals, or our efforts that lead to blessing and fulfillment. Our obedience does play a part as long as we remember that ultimately, "It is God which who worketh in you both to will and to do of his good pleasure" (Phil. 2:13). Paul identifies the goal for our lives as well as the means to attain that goal in 1 Thessalonians 5:23-24 when he says, "I pray God your whole spirit and soul and body be preserved blameless unto the coming of our Lord Jesus Christ. Faithful is he that calleth you, who also will do it."

There is certainly no question that Joseph lived a difficult life. Like Job before him, he was dealt blow after blow of ugly and unfair consequences which threatened to derail God's purpose for his life. Those threats, however, could only be effective if Joseph allowed his thoughts and views to be twisted by those circumstances over which he had no control. Instead, he chose to remember that God is in control and trust in those truths and promises that he could only see and access through the filter of his faith in God. That continuum of faith proved sufficient to keep his perspective right and God's purpose on track.

THE CHARACTER OF FORGIVENESS

ONE OF THE GREAT THEMES of Joseph's life was forgiveness. It is an incredible thought. Joseph endured more difficulty than many men have while maintaining a positive spirit and harboring no ill will toward those who mistreated him.

William Arthur Ward once wrote, "We are most like beasts when we kill. We are most like men when we judge. We are most like God when we forgive."[4] It was Alexander Pope who said, "To err is human, to forgive, divine."[5] Indeed, forgiveness, like love, is a cornerstone of God's character, a trait that we, as believers, are commanded to emulate.

Forgiveness is a conscious choice made by an individual who has been wronged, hurt, or offended to release the anger, resentment, and bitterness that they feel toward the one who caused their pain. It does not (and cannot) remove the responsibility for, eliminate the consequences of, or reverse the pain that was caused by the offense; nor can it guarantee the restoration of broken relationships, although that should always be the goal.

The elements of forgiveness are grounded in Scripture and demonstrated by God's character.

---

4   William Arthur Ward, "150 Quotes by William Arthur Ward," A-Z Quotes, accessed August 13, 2024, https://www.azquotes.com/author/15291-William_Arthur_ Ward?p=5#google_vignette.

5   Alexander Pope, *An Essay on Criticism, Poetry Foundation*, accessed August 5, 2024, https://www.poetryfoundation.org/articles/69379/an-essay-on-criticism.

FORGIVENESS IS ROOTED IN GOD'S LOVE

Moses was the man God had chosen to lead the children of Israel from Egypt into the Promised Land. But the Israelites were not exactly model followers. They repeatedly exasperated Moses and provoked God. So severe were their offenses that the Lord was ready to annihilate them and begin again with an entirely new nation (Num. 14:12). Moses responded by begging the Lord to pardon them, saying, "Pardon, I beseech thee, the iniquity of this people according unto the greatness of thy mercy, and as thou hast forgiven this people, from Egypt even until now" (Num. 14:19).

Notice that he appealed to God's "mercy" (or lovingkindness), noting that God had forgiven them many times already. In verse twenty, the Lord said, "I have pardoned according to thy word." You will notice that there were no conditions attached to the promise of forgiveness. The Lord did not demand that they repent, nor did He insist upon a waiting period to determine if their contrition was sincere. Moses didn't even require a sacrifice to be offered on their behalf. Because it is His nature to love and forgive His creation, God simply forgave His people. God's forgiveness always takes on the characteristics of His love: undeserved, unconditional, and unlimited.

When Jesus was dying on the cross, He offered a prayer on behalf of those who were crucifying Him, asking His Father to "forgive them, for they know not what they do" (Luke 23:34). The second part of that verse says, "And they parted his raiment, and cast lots." In essence, they ignored what He said. No one would insist that those men had received forgiveness, even though it had been given. It may seem like a very fine distinction; but Scripture clearly indicates that God's forgiveness is offered without conditions, while gaining forgiveness requires repentance and faith. To state it simply: God's forgiveness is motivated by His character and has already been provided for every man. The question is, and always has been, "Who is willing to receive it?" Joseph understood the magnitude of God's love for him, and that love motivated him to forgive his brothers just as God had forgiven him.

FORGIVENESS IS SECURED BY GOD'S SACRIFICE

Scripture tells us that forgiveness, or remission, comes through sacrifice: "And almost all things are by the law purged with blood, and without shedding of blood is no remission" (Heb. 9:22). Though we paid nothing for our forgiveness, it was far from free. In fact, without the sacrifice of our Redeemer, forgiveness wouldn't exist; and we would all be doomed. Our Savior sacrificed His purity to take upon Himself our sins; He sacrificed His power to set us free; and He gave His life to purchase our salvation. Sacrifice is always a necessary component of the process of forgiveness. God sacrificed the most valuable possession He had—His only begotten Son. We live because He died!

Our forgiveness must be accompanied by sacrifice as well. We must yield our pride, our desire for vengeance, and our need to approve what constitutes justice for our offender. Otherwise, our forgiveness is not complete.

Some people seem to think that Joseph had some kind of a spiritual filter that allowed him to endure the kind of trials that most men face without sacrifice. Joseph felt pain just as we do, and his suffering was just as real; but he chose to pay the price without complaint because he understood that the only people who find the path to genuine victory are those who are willing to forgive.

FORGIVENESS IS MEASURED BY GOD'S GRACE

God's grace and forgiveness are described as "riches" in Ephesians 1:7: "In whom we have redemption through his blood, the forgiveness of sins, according to the riches of his grace." How rich is God's grace? Many believers fail to understand the magnitude of God's forgiveness because they don't fully comprehend His grace. Two things are essential to that understanding: realizing the bitterness of God's hatred for sin and grasping the depth of His love for fallen man.

Romans 1:18 tells us that "the wrath of God is revealed from heaven against all ungodliness and unrighteousness of men." The word translated "wrath" has a connotation of "punitive justice." Because God is both righteous and just, He must judge sin—there is no alternative. God's hatred for sin is driven by His righteous character.

There is, however, another issue; sin also established a barrier between God and the man He created for fellowship. The path of communication was interrupted, and the man God loved had become lost to Him. Because of His love for man, God's eternal desire has always been to restore him to a place of fellowship. Man's sin, however, stood squarely in the way. The richness of God's grace was demonstrated by God's willingness to provide a sacrifice, making forgiveness available. The death of Christ on the cross made it possible for man to regain the righteousness necessary to satisfy God's holiness. God's willingness to sacrifice His only Son was driven by His love for man. How rich is God's grace? It is rich enough for God to sacrifice His only Son to pay for the sin He so bitterly hates to provide redemption for the fallen man He so deeply loves.

FORGIVENESS IS DEMONSTRATED BY GOD'S CHILDREN

Christians are commanded to "be ye kind one to another, tenderhearted, forgiving one another, even as God for Christ's sake hath forgiven you" (Eph. 4:32). It is astounding to learn how many believers actually think that they are somehow exempt from the biblical obligation to forgive others. They justify their position by citing the magnitude of their suffering, suggesting that some things are just "too painful" to forgive. "Besides," they might say, "are there not some who simply do not deserve forgiveness?" For these believers, forgiveness is impossible because they are driven by a longing for revenge, which they often insist is simply a desire for justice. If they do find it in their hearts to forgive it usually includes a condition ("I'll forgive you if . . . ") or a caveat ("I'll forgive you, but I will never forget.").

No one has ever suggested that forgiveness is easy. It requires surrendering our rights, acknowledging that life isn't always fair, and agreeing to let those who are genuinely guilty go free. As a consequence, innocent people suffer. It is the essence of injustice, exactly the opposite of what our flesh desires. Yet that is precisely how God has forgiven us.

Each of the questions below represents a specific challenge that must be overcome if a believer intends to obey the biblical command to forgive one another, "even as God for Christ's sake, hath forgiven" them.

- Must I forgive someone who is unwilling to repent? Granting forgiveness and receiving forgiveness are two separate issues. Forgiveness can be granted without the guilty party receiving it. The opposite scenario (receiving forgiveness without it being granted), however, is not possible.

- Can I forgive an individual who refuses to repent? Yes, because forgiveness, like love, is granted without conditions. Genuine forgiveness is offered solely at the discretion of the offended party, requiring nothing from the offender.

- Can an individual who refuses to repent be forgiven? No, receiving forgiveness requires repentance and faith (Luke 3:5).

- Must I forget what the offender has done? In most cases, forgetting is impossible. The Bible does not say that God has "forgotten" our sins. It does say that He will "remember [them] no more" (Heb. 10:17). We must choose to *forsake the memory* of those offenses that were committed against us. As long as we are keeping records, our forgiveness is incomplete.

- Must I surrender my right to be avenged? There is no "right to vengeance" to surrender. Romans 12:19 reminds us, "Dearly beloved, avenge not yourselves, but rather give place unto wrath: for it is written, Vengeance is mine; I will repay, saith the Lord." This has nothing to do with our legal system, nor does it affect God's principle of "sowing and reaping." It is simply not our place to determine the severity of judgment or carry out its sentence on those who have hurt us.

- Must I reconcile with my offender? Reconciliation is not an essential part of forgiveness. It is an additional step that often occurs as a result of the healing process. While the ultimate goal of forgiveness is always reconciliation, there are certain times when it cannot and should not happen.

  - We cannot reconcile with someone who is not available. There are occasions where the person we need to forgive is either dead or impossible to contact.

  - We cannot reconcile with someone who is unwilling to repent. They may be sincerely unaware of their offense or convinced that their actions were justified. In either case, from their perspective, they bear no guilt.

  - There are also times when it is unwise or impractical to reconcile, in spite of the fact that repentance may have occurred. In some cases, damage or pain from the offense is so severe that reconciliation is impossible, even when forgiveness has been sought and granted. The existence of new marriages that occurred after a relationship was destroyed through immorality is a good example of such a situation. Forgiveness should be given and received, but attempting to reconcile would usually be unwise.

    - Must I seek my offender's good? Jesus addressed this concern with explicit clarity in Matthew 5:43-44: "Ye have heard that it hath been said, Thou shalt love thy neighbour, and hate thine enemy. But I say unto you, Love your enemies, bless them that curse you, do good to them that hate you, and pray for them which despitefully use you, and persecute you." We are to "love," "bless," "do good to," and "pray for" those who are seeking to do us harm.

THE CONSEQUENCES OF UNFORGIVENESS

You may have heard a saying like this one: "Seeking vengeance is like drinking rat poison and then waiting for the rat to die." When we choose not to forgive, we are sentencing ourselves to a slow, ugly death. Ephesians 4:31 identifies six spiteful character traits—"bitterness, and wrath, and anger, and clamour, and evil speaking . . . with all malice"—which are indicative of an unforgiving heart.

We all know people who are like that, and we would emphatically agree that they are no fun to be around. They usually don't even like themselves. Obsessive in their pursuit of revenge, their lives are one-dimensional; and every circumstance is viewed through the filter of their ruthless mission. The sad truth is that achieving their goal will not bring satisfaction or relief. The pain and damage will remain, as will the ugly attitude. The only thing that can provide the freedom they are seeking is a willingness to forgive their offender.

The other, more significant consequence of choosing not to forgive is the loss of the blessing and guidance of the Spirit of God. Ephesians 4:30 says that the Holy Spirit is grieved when forgiveness is rejected. Matthew 6:14-15 says that an individual with an unforgiving spirit will not receive forgiveness from his Heavenly Father. Unforgiveness damages our relationship with God.

The stipulation of Scripture is that we are to forgive "even as God for Christ's sake has forgiven" us (Eph. 4:32). That includes rooting our forgiveness in love, securing our forgiveness by personal sacrifice, and offering that forgiveness with the same measure of grace that we have received from our

God. Though not easy, it is commanded; and those who obey are rewarded with a sense of peace, a spirit of freedom, and an enduement of power that allows them to endure unbelievable challenges with joy and enables them to do remarkable things in their service for the Lord.

Joseph was that kind of man.

PRINCIPLES OF RECONCILIATION

RECONCILIATION IS A BIBLICAL REQUIREMENT in successfully re-establishing a damaged relationship that is often overlooked. While Joseph had, without question, forgiven his brothers very early in his life, his brothers' complete reconciliation with Joseph did not occur until after their father died. While forgiveness is a part of reconciliation, it is only a part. Reconciliation goes a good bit further.

To understand biblical reconciliation, we must understand the full context of our salvation. Far too many people view salvation primarily as a way to avoid paying for their sins, meaning they will not have to spend eternity tormented by the flames of Hell. The more pleasant consequence of that reality is that they will spend eternity in the presence of their Savior in a place that has been prepared specifically for believers—a place where peace, joy, and harmony rule. What makes that possible is redemption. Without redemption, reconciliation is impossible.

Redemption is what provides payment for our sins and gives us the righteousness required to be reconciled to God. When Jesus died upon the cross, He took our sins upon Himself; and when we trusted Him as our Savior, He gave us His righteousness, something we did not deserve and could never earn. Redemption is just one of three very important transactions that occur precisely at the moment of salvation.

Another of those transactions is regeneration. Regeneration has to do with us receiving new life—that is, everlasting life that likewise provides a pathway to reconciliation. Regeneration in Scripture is described in this way: "And you hath he quickened, who were dead in trespasses and sins" (Eph. 2:1). The word "quickened" means to be "made alive." You will notice in the verse that we are described as being "dead" in trespasses and sins. We change from being spiritually dead to being alive in Christ when converted. It is not possible to reconcile with a dead person.

The third transaction is reconciliation. Reconciliation has to do with relationship. Colossians 1:21-22 explains the concept: "And you, that were sometime alienated and enemies in your mind by wicked works, yet now hath he reconciled In the body of his flesh through death, to present you holy and unblamable and unreproveable in his sight." The primary purpose of our salvation is to reconcile us to God. It was our sin that separated us from God. It was our sin that caused us to die spiritually. Reconciliation means that the barrier that separated us from our God and caused us to die spiritually has been removed. We are made holy, unblamable, and unreprovable in His sight. That means we can come freely into God's presence—without guilt, without fear, and with complete trust in Him. We are no longer alienated from Him because our relationship has been restored. We have been reconciled to God.

This truth is illustrated for us in a powerful way in Scripture. Old Testament believers had a far different view of salvation than we have today. They were looking forward to the arrival of a Messiah Who would provide the promised freedom of redemption. We look back at the turning point of man's salvation, the coming of the promised Messiah Who paid our sin debt on the cross, providing redemption for every individual who would believe in Him.

Since the death of Christ was yet future for Old Testament believers, God established a ceremonial system of worship that would allow them to demonstrate their faith. But the barrier between them and their God was very real, even though they believed in the coming Messiah. Because of the barrier, they had no open communication with their God. They offered sacrifices to show their love and express their faith, and God sent prophets to give them instruction and guidance. Communication with God was stilted and difficult because of the barrier.

The reality of the barrier was easy to see in their place of worship, a temple that provided a place for priests to offer sacrifices to God on behalf of the people. The temple was divided into three parts. The outer court was an open courtyard without a roof that served as an entrance to the enclosed portion of the temple. The enclosed portion had two parts, the Holy Place and the Holy of Holies. The two areas were separated by a very thick curtain. Inside the Holy of Holies was the ark of the covenant, which contained the covenant (the Ten Commandments). It was the most sacred piece of furniture in the temple. And atop the ark rested the Mercy Seat, which was the place where God met with man to deal with man's sin.

Only one person was allowed to go into the Holy of Holies. The high priest went in once a year to sprinkle blood obtained from a flawless lamb on the Mercy Seat to atone for the sins of the people. If anyone else entered the Holy of Holies, he would die instantly. Why? Because of his sin. He was not redeemed. He was still dead in his sin. And he had crossed the barrier or crossed into the presence of God while still in his sin. The curtain was the physical barrier in the temple; the obstacle that made it impossible for unredeemed man to enter the presence of the absolutely pure, righteous, holy God of eternity.

Skip forward several hundred years to an event with which we are all so familiar. Christ has been nailed to a cross and is hanging in meekness and disgrace between two common thieves. He is there unjustly, having been falsely accused and condemned; and it is our sin that has put Him there. He begins to speak, and His words demonstrate His compassion—first, for those who were causing His pain (Luke 23:34), then for the thief hanging beside Him who confessed his sin (Luke 23:43). He took time to care for His mother (John 19:26-27).

Then, as the end drew near, the Bible tells us that he uttered the words, "It is finished," and gave up the ghost (John 19:30). What happened next was one of those heart-stopping moments that makes you realize, as did those who were watching, that this man who was hanging on the cross was no ordinary man but that He was, indeed, the Son of God. The Bible tells us that there was darkness over the face of the earth for three hours (Mark 15:33). There was then an earthquake violent enough to cause the rocks to split open. And finally, over in the temple, the veil, the curtain, the barrier that for hundreds of years had separated the common sinful man from the place where God met with man on earth, was ripped in two, and the path was cleared for man to come into the presence of God (Matt. 27:51). Man's guilt could then be removed, his fear eradicated, and complete trust established so that man could be reconciled to his maker.

These principles are clearly demonstrated in the life of Joseph's brothers as they responded to his forgiveness. Forgiveness is always the responsibility of the offended party in a damaged relationship. Reconciliation depends on the guilty party's heart attitude in response to that forgiveness.

GENERAL PRINCIPLES OF RECONCILIATION

1. Reconciliation is an attempt, using biblical principles, to remove the barriers between the two parties in a damaged relationship, thereby restoring the peace and unity necessary for the relationship to flourish and prosper.

2. Reconciliation requires the participation of both parties in the damaged relationship. Because the basic nature of reconciliation is to remove the barrier between two people or parties, both parties must be involved. Every case involves an offended party as well as the offender. If there are multiple offenses involving

both parties, each barrier must be dealt with and removed, eliminating guilt and fear and restoring trust.

3. Forgiveness is the responsibility of the offended party. Confession is the primary responsibility of the offender.

4. Reconciliation with an offended party who refuses to forgive his offender is impossible.

5. Reconciliation with an offender who refuses to acknowledge his offense is not possible.

6. Reconciliation with an offender who refuses to accept a sincere offer of forgiveness from the party he has offended is not possible.

7. An offended party can avoid the destructive forces of bitterness and resentment by forgiving his offender, even if his offender chooses not to receive it.

8. An offender cannot overcome the utter despair of guilt and fear without reaching a point of reconciliation with the party he has offended.

For reconciliation to be complete, three things must occur:
- Guilt must be eliminated.
- Fear must be eradicated.
- Trust must be established.

Joseph's brothers lived for years with the guilt of what they had done, fearing Joseph and anticipating repayment for their sin. Though they confessed after the silver cup was found in Benjamin's sack, they did not believe Joseph's promise of forgiveness. As a result, the guilt was not eliminated; and reconciliation was not achieved. It was only after their father died that they finally accepted Joseph's forgiveness. At that time, their guilt was removed; their fear disappeared; and they were finally able to trust their brother and find the peace, joy, and freedom that true reconciliation provides.

BIBLIOGRAPHY

Merriam-Webster. S.v. "perspective (n.)." Accessed August 5, 2024. https://www. merriam-webster.com/dictionary/perspective.

Pope, Alexander. *An Essay on Criticism.* Poetry Foundation. Accessed August 5, 2024. https://www.poetryfoundation.org/articles/69379/ an-essay-on-criticism.

Twain, Mark. "Forbidden." Twainquotes.com. Accessed August 5, 2024. http:// www.twainquotes.com/Forbidden.html.

Ward, William Arthur. "150 Quotes by William Arthur Ward." A-Z Quotes. Accessed August 13, 2024, https://www.azquotes.com/ author/15291-William_Arthur_Ward?p=5#google_vignette.

ABOUT THE AUTHOR

TERRY HYMAN PASTORED TRINITY BAPTIST Church in Centerville, Georgia, for almost twenty-one years. His ministry spans more than fifty years and includes a number of churches in the Southeast. He is the author of *Studies in the Minor Prophets*, written to help church members understand and apply the eternal truth found in those "uninteresting" and "impractical" prophecies, and *David: The Godly Heart of a Sinful Man*. He also posts frequently at www.terryhyman.net. He and his wife, Myra, live in Waxhaw, North Carolina, near their three sons and ten grandchildren.

For more information about Terry Hyman and *Joseph*, please visit:

www.terryhyman.net

@pastortwhyman

www.linkedin.com/in/terry-hyman-68016843

Ambassador International's mission is to magnify the Lord Jesus Christ and promote His Gospel through the written word.

We believe through the publication of Christian literature, Jesus Christ and His Word will be exalted, believers will be strengthened in their walk with Him, and the lost will be directed to Jesus Christ as the only way of salvation.

For more information about
AMBASSADOR INTERNATIONAL
please visit:

www.ambassador-international.com

@AmbassadorIntl

www.facebook.com/AmbassadorIntl

Thank you for reading this book. Please consider leaving us a review on your social media, favorite retailer's website, Goodreads or Bookbub, or our website.

WONDERLURE
BEING LURED INTO THE WONDER OF GOD'S PRESENCE
JASON LAWSON

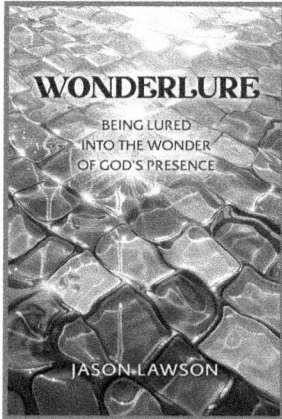

Wonderlure will take you on a journey of discovering more about Emmanuel Who will never leave you, the Lamb of God Who takes away your sins, the True Vine which grows joy, peace, and love in you, the Cornerstone that lays the line of truth, the Father Who is so proud of you, the Messiah Who can't wait to come back and take you home, and the Sunrise Who sees through your darkness and makes it light. As you read through this book, allow yourself to be lured into the wonder of His presence.

Throughout her years serving alongside her husband, who pastored Southside Baptist Church (now Fellowship Greenville) in Greenville, South Carolina, for over thirty years, Elizabeth Rice Handford has had the opportunity to touch many lives with her daily devotionals. In her new devotional, *Fullness of Joy*, take a dive into one hundred of Libby's devotionals, compiled from a look back through her writings and life experiences.

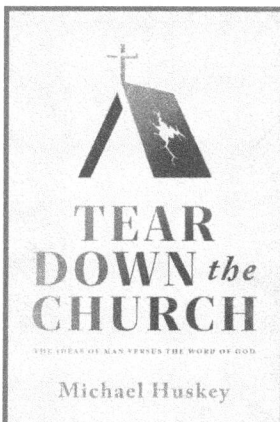

FULLNESS OF JOY
ONE HUNDRED DEVOTIONS TO BRING YOU INTO GOD'S PRESENCE
ELIZABETH RICE HANDFORD

TEAR DOWN *the* **CHURCH**
THE IDEAS OF MAN VERSES THE WORD OF GOD
Michael Huskey

One of the biggest issues the Church faces is the influence of extrabiblical sources—what Spurgeon called "the downgrade." In *Tear Down the Church*, Michael Huskey examines the problems that result when the Church strays from keeping the Scripture central to its teaching and culture. Addressing leadership in the body of believers as well as leadership in the family, each chapter guides, challenges and exhorts readers to set aside false ideas that impede God's intentions for His children and to return to the Truth found in the Bible.

www.ingramcontent.com/pod-product-compliance
Lightning Source LLC
Chambersburg PA
CBHW071753090426
42737CB00012B/1807